Woman *in the* Locker Room

An Alaskan Woman's Journey for Change

Maggie Holeman

PO Box 221974 Anchorage, Alaska 99522-1974
books@publicationconsultants.com—www.publicationconsultants.com

ISBN 978-1-59433-576-1
eISBN 978-1-59433-577-8
Library of Congress Catalog Card Number: 2015959977

Manufactured in the United States of America.

Dedications

This book is dedicated to the memory of my parents.
I hope they have found peace wherever they may be...

And to my two children, Joshua and Brittany.
You gave me a reason to find happiness.

To Joseph – my forever friend.

To Gail – Sisters of the Forest

This is dedicated to my sister, Virginia. Although the violence
of our past separated us, the search for its reasoning brought
us together as adults. You are my hero.

And to all the men and women who work in Emergency
Services. Without their vigilance over us, it would be
a darker world.

Never "for the sake of peace and quiet"
deny your own experience or convictions.
—Dag Hammarskjold

Acknowledgements

To Shawn Butler, thank you for your technical support with the computers. Without your help, my computer would have several bullet holes in the screen.

To Andrea Petitfils, thank you for your editing and suggestions. They were excellent.

To Micheal Holmes, although our lives crossed only shortly, the impact of your words were everlasting.

To William Mulcahey, a 25-year veteran and Captain of the FDNY who gave me my first chance to be published through his magazine Aviation Fire Journal. Without your encouragement and words of affirmation, I may have never continued.

To Carlton Erikson and Jim Fleming, former co-workers who gave me insight and technical assistance. I am thankful for our re-acquaintances. Both your patience and ability to edit what I "think" as well as what I "write."

To James Misko, my mentor, friend and B&B guest. Thank you for listening and guiding me through some of my worst fears. You are an excellent teacher.

To Carol Mousley, thank you for reading and correcting my stories. You gave me hope I could do this.

To Charol Messenger, a writer and editor. I had problems with time lines and tenses and you gently guided me through a web of confusion to an organized text.

To Joe Knyszek, thank you for the title.

To Evan Swensen, publisher and a patient man.

Prologue

"Maggie, don't come in here," Sergeant Siegmann insisted. "You really don't need to see this."

I moved him aside as he attempted to block my entrance to the fire-station stall. The sight of the five opened body bags lying on the floor seared a gruesome image into my memory. A lifetime of shelving pictures, tucking them into the back of my mind, trying to suppress what I was seeing. Still I remember them. And the smell of death. These were once men—walking, talking, and living. Now they lay in body bags, mutilated. Some missing half their heads, their brains exposed; eyeballs dangling from what were once their sockets. Blood-soaked clothing ripped and shredded as though a monster grabbed, then tossed them into the air like string puppets. They lay heavy under their lifeless mass—their substance gone.

The stark reality of death staring me in the face. I had never seen anything like this before. And when I walked out, I hoped I would never see anything like it again.

This story is about change. Changing the rules, changing attitudes, conceptions, traditions and roles. It's about spirit, drive, tenacity, independence, and human growth. And it's about bravery. Not only in the sense of our chosen careers, but in the sense of accepting personal strengths and the ability to let go.

Introduction

I was born in the Territory of Alaska in 1951, at that time dad had already been in Alaska on and off for twenty-one years.

My father was born Ben Rapley Holeman on March 26, 1908, in Memphis, Tennessee. His father had been a judge. But dad was a maverick and left for Alaska at the age of 22 with a brother, one of five. Dad worked as a civilian and helped to build Ft. Richardson army base. Then the gold fever lured him to Nebesna, Alaska, where he worked for four years at one of the largest gold-producing mines in the 1930s. Although his brother finally left Alaska, dad remained until he died.

My parents married in Seattle, Washington in 1937. My mother's life turned from having household help and upscale social parties to living in a one-room cabin with no running water at the Nebesna Gold Mine in the Wrangell Mountains of Alaska and more than two hundred miles away from any real civilization.

Alaska is a rugged place to live, with harsh winters and desolate remoteness. The Athabaskan Indians gave my mother two huskies to protect her from the bears during her daily trek from her one-room cabin to the gold mine to give dad his lunch. What an adventurous and strong spirit she must have had to cope with such conditions. My parents left Nebesna in 1940 when the mine was closed at the beginning of WWII when the price of gold plummeted. Dad worked the next thirty-two years with the Federal Aviation Agency (FAA out of Anchorage) which was then called Civil Aeronautics Authority (CAA).

I can still see my thin father sitting in his dark-green vinyl recliner in the corner next to the double-pane windows in our

Anchorage house. It was *his* chair and no one else was allowed to sit in it. On the days he traveled with his job as a maintenance inspector with the FAA, his chair would remain empty.

Dad was one of the first white men to speak the Athabaskan language fluently in Alaska, even before it was a written language. On the nights when he drank his whiskey, his legs crossed in his green recliner and chanting Athabaskan, I didn't appreciate the language. In fact, I hated it because he only chanted it when he was intoxicated. Beside him in the green chair were his un-filtered Lucky Strikes and an ice-filled glass of amber-colored destruction, which he constantly refilled until the spirits consumed him into an unconscious state.

Margaret Loomis David, my mother, was born in Mobile, Alabama on December 25, 1912, and had always been robbed of gift-giving extravaganzas. We tried to make her feel special by wrapping presents in birthday paper as well as Christmas paper, and baking her birthday cake.

I remember her crooked smile and red lipstick, her gray hair and dark eyes. The scent of her perfume, Shalimar, stayed with me for years after her death. I can still see her sitting on the end of our couch, cigarette smoke wafting in the air, her left leg securely tucked under her. Once a week my mom would visit the beauty parlor just up the street to have her hair shampooed and curled. The bounce and color in her hair was eventually replaced with bobby-pins and hairspray and blue dye.

When the three of us kids came home from elementary school we tossed our school books onto the fireplace mantle, wired from our day and desperate for play. But our excitement would disturb her peace, and our world would become darkened like hers. Only moments after arriving into the 1953 flat-roofed house my father had built, we felt her damaged spirit as she sat there sipping on her whiskey, her near daily ritual. Her empty words "How was your day?" were a vacuous question.

The population of Anchorage in 1951, the year I was born, was 47,000. Located 61 degrees north latitude, it is just north of Oslo, Norway and St. Petersburg, Russia. It is a subarctic climate with the Northern Boreal Forest. Anchorage is located at the base of the Chugach Mountains and alongside the treacherous Cook Inlet waters of South Central Alaska.

We lived one block south of the city limits in Anchorage, Alaska, on 16th Avenue between L and K streets. It was a nice middle-class neighborhood with lots of kids. Almost everyone knew each other.

I'm the youngest of four children, my older brother, Benjamin being 11 years my senior. Next in line was my sister, Virginia, two years my senior, then my other brother, Richard (nicknamed Tiger), one year older.

Benjamin was a handsome young man of eighteen when he left home. He had red, curly hair, dark eyes, and, like me, his freckles came out in the sunlight. He was tall, too, and strong as an ox. Although he was quick to laugh, he also had a temper that could explode unpredictably. Mostly, I was scared of him. He made up a game called "sissy-fight." Those sissies weak enough to falter were called a denotation of a girls' makeup—demeaning, like you're nothing, less than nothing.

Benji taught the rest of us how to fight, something he evidently had already learned early living under our roof. Maybe he focused his anger on us for the injustice he felt was happening to him. And, although I don't know much about him maybe he was in survival mode like the rest of us.

I was seven in the winter of 1958 when my big brother left home for good. I remember the very moment he left because I knew he was taking, in part, a sense of our security with him. Only because he protected us sometimes when the violence escalated to a point we couldn't get away.

Our home was like a dormant fuse that led to an unpredictable explosion. Some spark would light it but you never knew when or what caused that to happen. The fuse was connected to my parents, my sister, both brothers, and me, intertwined in a cobweb of destruction. Our lives were like living in a war zone: you knew the bomb was going off but you didn't know when so you always had to be prepared. We were all guilty and, after a period of time, we were all willing to light the fuse.

I had been awake for hours, knowing he was leaving early in the morning and I didn't want to miss saying goodbye. I occupied my time in the dark basement playing finger games – ittsy wittsy spider – and humming familiar safe sounds—*Somewhere Over the Rainbow*—to keep myself awake.

Although my eyes were adjusted to the darkness, I only saw a muted shadow as he started up the stairs next to my bed. I heard his hand slide against the wooden railing, feeling his way up and my pretend world stopped.

I called out softly, "Benji, are you leaving?"

He stopped on the creaky, wooden steps. "Shhh," he said, "Go to sleep." Then he disappeared.

And that was that.

Chapter One

1961

One particularly disruptive evening when my parents had both turned on my sister, Virginia, she had telephoned our brother, Benji. In the trembling voice of a 13-year old child, she cupped the receiver of the phone located in our basement so no one else could hear. Then she pleaded, "Benji. Please help me."

Virginia was delicate in stature. With her lily-white skin and black wavy hair she had the appearance of Snow White. She was tall but thin. She was smart, too and popular. I always envied her having so many friends.

Following the phone call, all solid 6-foot 3-inches of Benji, came to her rescue. Explanation in our world didn't exist, and Benji wasn't looking for one. He heard and understood the distress call. He burst through the door and when the door flew open, he could see my sister's face was smeared with blood from being smashed into the kitchen counter by her abusers, knocking her front tooth out. He worked his way into position and drew back with a fist and punched my dad in the face. My dad's body collapsed into a crumpled heap. My mother was also the abuser and I was surprised and relieved he didn't also hit her. It had taken both my parents to *control* my sister as they thrust her face into the hardwood counter in our kitchen. She had "mouthed off" to them, expressing a hatred for the alcohol.

Hiding behind the couch in a near fetal position, I watched as the events unfolded. Behind my bunker of safety, the war raged in front of me. My dad's body splayed in unconsciousness, the room echoing with screams. Voices pitched, hands waving in defiance threatening to strike, spit spewing from the mouths whose words were the loudest.

Bracing my hands against my ears to keep the bad people out, I saw the hard candy stuck on my father's tongue. What if he choked? I hesitated to step out, risking having the violence turn on me, to remove the candy.

Benji took my sister with him and left the house.

Then the police came. Our real saviors. I'd seen them before in our house. They always came in twos. And although our family dynamic would return to its dysfunctional array as soon as the police left, their presence brought an impregnable net of safety. No one could hurt while they were under our roof.

The police drew the attention of mom and with that I ran to dad's body to pluck the candy from his mouth. I didn't want anyone to feel pain. Not even the abusers.

As I regained my position behind the big sofa to watch the repetitive story of turmoil unfold, I felt thankful this go-around didn't include me.

I was so wrong about that.

1974

Fire Station One Anchorage International Airport

"How do you compensate for not being a man?"

—Question asked in my first oral board interview with Airport Police/Fire.

I stood alone as the first woman hired at Anchorage International Airport, Airport Police and Fire Department, State of Alaska. A department of 86 men.

The first day of my employment in 1974 at age 23 I proudly stood at roll call, dwarfed among 15 other officers on my shift facing my first obstacle: discrimination and harassment.

At 7:45, Alaska's November morning sun was tucked away somewhere but we wouldn't see it for another two hours. The north wind whistled in the darkness behind the brick walls of the fire station.

My gray shirt, black pants, black belt, and plain black boots conformed to the assigned uniform for a new recruit. It made me stand out as a rookie against the handsome blue uniforms of the men. Regardless of the drab outfit, my boots were spit polished, creases down the middle of my men's black pants and military creases in my man's shirt.

Captain Grant's black, beady eyes shifted back and forth as he critically searched for faults among the sixteen of us on the day shift. A buzz of curiosity rolled through the kitchen where roll call was about to begin.

Standing side by side, we impatiently awaited instructions from the captain, and began to quiet down.

From behind his podium, Captain Grant's eyes stopped on me. "We have a new recruit here." His tight lips barely broke space as he talked.

Flushed with embarrassment, I quickly averted my eyes to the red door that separated the men's locker room from one of the three entrances into the kitchen. I concentrated on the cement block wall at the end of the row of gray lockers, which tunneled down the narrow hall.

The men took the captain's word as permission to gawk at me. His tone of voice gave them a reason to disagree with my being hired. Turning their attention to me, they muttered their disapproval, shook their heads. Dismantled in a matter of seconds. First day, first minutes. Alienated.

How dare I step across that line?

But I did. And I was in.

"Sergeant Moss," barked the captain, "get her a uniform jacket and hardware, (gun, handcuffs, holster) and assign her a locker. Just get her familiar with the area today. She'll start training tomorrow."

Despite being ostracized, I was excited. I was drawn to the unconventional/non-traditional world. This career track would make me prove to myself if I had any worth.

Captain Grant of the Airport Police and Fire Department quickly discarded my presence. The sergeant went on to relay the previous shift's pertinent information. After roll call, the men began to leave for their day-shift assignments. The captain moved away from the podium, grasping his aluminum crutches. I watched him maneuver down the tiled hall floor to his office at the rear of the locker room.

After he turned right at the first corridor Jack Moss said, "Come on, Maggie. I'll show you around."

He guided me toward the truck stalls. "I'll go get you a uniform jacket in the back here," he said in his soft voice. "In the meantime, here is your locker."

There were five stall bays for the trucks and between stall one and two was a row of lockers. This was an over-flow dressing area because the main locker room, which was warm and enclosed, was full. The string of lockers I was to dress in was wide open; the only privacy I had was if the fire truck was still in the stall giving some protection behind me.

The cold, drafty truck bays sent a shiver up my spine as I faced my new dressing room.

All of my uniforms, both police and fire (everyone did double-duty), along with all fire equipment assigned to me, would be stored in this six-foot, four-foot-wide locker.

Jack returned with my jacket.

"Where are the bathrooms, Jack?"

"Guess you'll be using the same one as us," he stammered, "in the men's locker room." He looked away with embarrassment.

I understood immediately. I would be dressing and undressing in the open with all the men. I would be using the toilet with them as well. This is the way it's always been and this is the way it will be. No extra provisions: make her fit in. Or get rid of her.

The bathroom was down the first aisle of the men's locker room. The outer door was propped securely opened. I scanned the room. Two sinks to the left, a large mirror above. Across from them, two standard toilet stalls. Directly ahead, a urinal. To the right, two shower stalls.

As I entered this testosterone world, a faint but distinct odor hovered in the air from a sanitizing disk. The vinyl shower curtains were torn; several clips hung on rusted metal rods. I pulled the curtain back on the nearest shower. The incandescent light reflected years of build-up from sweaty, dirty bodies where the men had washed after working a fire or being involved in a police altercation. Even Clorox would not dissolve the embedded filth encircling the drain.

I walked to a toilet stall and closed the door behind me. As I pulled my trousers down, I felt exposed; there was a gap between the door and the wall.

I wasn't surprised by the arrangement set up for my *inconvenience* but not worth filing a complaint. Blurting out what I thought was unjust could easily end my new career before it started. So I held my tongue—except for a small bite now and then, just enough to irritate the rule makers.

"Get her in here and let's measure her for size," Captain Grant ordered Officer John Tibor.

John found me reading the department's Standard Operating Procedures (SOP) manual, familiar to any government agency. I was in the kitchen with two other officers.

"The captain wants to see you," John said. "His office is in the back of the men's locker room. Come on, I'll show you."

I followed him obediently.

As we entered the locker room, he announced, "Woman in the locker room! Woman in the locker room!"

The men who were changing quickly covered up. I wondered would they announce, "Men between the fire trucks," when they came into my dressing area?

John Tibor left me alone with Captain Grant. "Do you know your hat size?" the captain snarled as I entered his cramped, small office, a space he shared with the fire captain who was not present.

Sitting behind his desk cluttered with paperwork, Captain Grant repeated himself. "Do you know your hat size or not?"

"No, sir," I announced carefully. But I couldn't leave it there, and added, "I don't know it because I've never worn a man's hat."

Captain Grant glared at me for my impudence.

"Look at these." He pointed to several makeshift cardboard hat cutouts.

I put them on my head feeling like a fool. "This one," I concluded. Size 6-7/8.

"I'll have to order it," he growled, "We don't keep them in stock that small." He turned away and reached for something under his desk. A shadow cast across his dark complexion through the only window in the office. "Did you get a jacket?" he asked.

"Yes, but it's a size 42. I wear a 36," I held my breath, anticipating his adversarial reaction. I knew he was going to have to order everything.

He turned toward me. Trying to control his agitation, he answered, "I'll see what I can do." Then he dismissed me with a wave.

But I didn't leave. "Captain Grant, when I use the bathroom, do I announce myself as 'Woman in the locker room?'"

He turned away with tightly pursed lips. Instead of answering my confrontational question, he changed the subject and disintegrated me with a stare. "Hair regulations state you must have your hair above the collar. It's for your safety and the ability to seal an air mask. Any more questions?" He put both of his strong hands on his desk and leaned forward testing, my fortitude.

I nodded without answering. I already kept my naturally curly hair short to control it, but it was just below the collar. As I left the men's locker room, I yelled, "Woman in the locker room! Woman in the locker room!"

Chapter Two

1960

With the excitement of Christmas the next morning, the three of us kids gathered around the Christmas tree the evening before, giggling, playing, and making noise. Mom and dad sat at their usual places, drinking.

"Do you know who Santa Claus really is?" Mom asked the three of us.

I wasn't ready for this answer besides thinking he was a nice, jolly fat man that brought me presents. This is the man who helps me forget evil.

I piped up immediately, "I know! He's the man with the white beard and wears a red and white suit and has a sled…and why are you asking us this? You know who he is."

In my mother's stewed state, she pointed to my dad. "That's Santa Claus." She said it with conviction. "There is no man with a white beard and wears red and white suit and has a sled." Still continuing to point in my father's direction, she added, "This is the man who pays for all your presents."

It took me a minute to understand the information but I didn't believe it. I didn't want to believe it.

Then, without warning, our pretend Santa Claus got up from his chair and cut all the Christmas lights with a wire cutter. Gone. Poof. Dark. That fast and the evening was over as we ran downstairs. No more Santa Claus. No more Christmas lights. No more explanation.

I was nine years old at the time and had lain awake all night thinking we weren't going to have Christmas lights in the morning. So I'd gotten up, found my dad's soldering iron, plugged it in and waited for it to heat. I didn't realize at that time I had singed a burn mark into the wooden table that would remind me in the future my quest to save the Christmas lights.

Then I stripped two wires like I had seen him do before on other occasions, twist them together, and then hit it with a soldering iron. Smug in my convictions that this was how it was done, I plugged the wire end into the wall receptacle and blew the electricity in the entire upstairs! I was so petrified that I just stood there motionless in the dark house in my pajamas with my mouth opened, unable to understand what happened or how I could fix it. Although the house was cool, I was hot from fear. The possible repercussions would keep me up the remainder of the night. I abandoned my efforts to go to sleep.

Christmas morning came and before I got up, my dad had fixed the Christmas tree lights by changing a circuit breaker.

He never confronted me. He never said anything.

Santa Claus was dead.

1975

"Anyone home?" I yelled at the door of my parent's house. I banged my boots against the door jamb to knock the snow loose before I stepped inside. Then I slipped them off before walking into the living area.

The afternoon light was already fading and the darkness encroaching. My shift had ended at 4 p.m. and my parent's house was only about seven miles from the airport.

"Come in, Maggie. We're both here," answered mom.

As I walked into the living room, two lamps softly illuminated the living room that reflected the natural knotty pine paneling. I found my parents in the living room.

I could see my mom's dark eyes search for me as I came in behind her.

She sat at the corner of the couch, her favorite place, with her left leg tucked securely under her butt. I had stopped by to see what the plans for Christmas were.

As I entered the room my eyes naturally went to the table nearest to my mother to locate the glass of whiskey. And there it was—as usual—the glass filled with anger, pain and vacancy. No matter how many times I had seen this picture, I couldn't control my feelings of loss, what the glass of whiskey had taken from me. It took my mother. In the past, I would find myself irritating my mom, making her mad at me because I was so mad at her for abandoning me both emotionally and physically. She was empty, consumed by the amber liquid that put her in another state of mind. Somewhere away from us kids.

My dad sat to my mom's right, in the corner. He sat in his favorite green vinyl reclining chair next to the large plate-glass windows that faced south. To his left on the table the blue smoke from his lit cigarette drifted upwards, the unfiltered Lucky Strike tilting on the edge of an ashtray already filled with used butts. His half-empty glass of whiskey sat next to the ashtray.

As I entered the living room, my dad picked up his whiskey glass and I could hear the ice cubes clink together—a sound I had learned to hate. I caught his eyes but only briefly.

"So, what's the plan for Christmas?" I asked casually.

"We thought we could open presents the day before over here," mom said, trying to accommodate my work schedule.

I would be working on Christmas Day. The holiday fell on my regular work day, so I would have to work it.

Shift rotations involved changing shifts and days off every twenty-eight days. That gave the officers the chance to experience all three shifts and gain from the more rounded exposure. All the new rookies were making that rotation according to the posted schedule. However, for some reason I was being kept on day shift; I wasn't rotating with the other rookies.

Sullen, I didn't care if I missed Christmas.

I stated flatly, "So, I'll be here after work on Christmas Eve."

Then I changed the subject. I was anxious about the upcoming fire academy, even though it was still three months away.

I said to my mom, "I have a fire academy and a police academy coming up in late February or March. I'm a little nervous about the fire academy."

I thought to myself that I kept in fair physical condition, and my adolescent fat had long disappeared, but fighting a fire was going to take enormous strength. If I wasn't strong or brave enough for this part of the career, it would simply be over.

"Are you sure you want to do this?" Mom asked as she stirred the ice in the whiskey glass with her finger.

I sat at the round table that I had singed so many years ago as I faced her. It had two chairs and was the table at which my parents ate every meal together—away from us. The four of us kids would cram ourselves into the small kitchen, often making way too much noise laughing and playing games. We never ate one meal with our parents.

Mom asked again, "Are you sure you want to do this?"

Maybe if she hadn't been drinking, I would have pursued the question. However, her sip of whiskey turned my attitude to defiance. "Positive. I've never been so sure of anything before."

The dim lighting cast a shadow across my mother's aging face. Her brown eyes had lost their luster. Because I was born late in their lives, I'd never known either of them without gray hair.

My parents' voices became muted in the back of my head as a good memory edged its way to the front of my mind. Behind the couch my mom sat in is a strip of linoleum floor covering. I thought about times mom would put paste wax down, then the three of us, in our stocking feet, would come running from the hallway and slide onto the paste wax, buffing it with our feet. What a blast that was! We could edge a little further each time as we buffed in the wax and the floor became shiny and slippery. I'm amazed none of us went head first into the floor.

The thought brought a smile to my face; something from the past.

Bringing me back to reality, my dad asked, "So, how many uniforms do you wear now?" He took a draw from his cigarette then blew the smoke directly in front of him.

Having lived through a chaotic and volatile childhood, I was drawn to some sort of disciplinary setting with boundaries. So, I took the basic military aptitude tests and had joined the Army National Guard in 1973.

"Three, dad," I answered curtly. "Police, Fire and Army."

He laughed, brushing away my life. The emptiness of his response burrowed a target into my heart. As if all I had tried to do with my life were pointless and meaningless. It was time for me to leave.

My abrupt departure came with no explanation. "Tell me about Christmas later, I have to go."

Unlike in my youth, as an adult I was free to walk out that door. As a child, I felt trapped—somewhere I didn't want to be. It was suffocating. Suffocation comes to a child when she has to endure the violence, whether it was aimed at her or a sibling or even the other parent. It magnified the sense she was alone.

As I drove home to my small efficiency apartment on the west side of town, the conversation with my parents replayed in my mind. Why wasn't my dad proud of me? I had entered the aviation field, thinking we could have some kind of connection. He had been an inspector of runway lighting and maintenance for the FAA and had recently retired after thirty-two years.

I stepped out of my red Valiant and into the coldness of the afternoon that slapped my face. I climbed the stairs to my second-story apartment, and opened the door to the part of my life I had purposely chosen: living alone. A certain sense of control. After eighteen years of living with my parents under the façade of a normal family setting, as an adult I welcomed the silence and to live without fear.

Chapter Three

1961

When her fists hit my small body, I curled into the fetal position and tightened my grip on the bed covers. I was sick.

"I hate you! I hate you! I'm sick of you being sick!" And her fists came down again and again. I told myself, "Don't puke, whatever you do, don't puke." If I do, I'd be lying all over it. And my mother's fists came again. I was glad the covers, which were over my entire body including my head, had caused a barrier that eased some of the blows that pounded on me. I needed to go to my "safe place" in my mind. And I did until it was over. I was ten years old.

1975

"As long as I am a Captain, there will *never* be a woman hired."

—Told to me second hand by an officer before my first oral interview. Capt. Grant was on the Review Board. I flunked.

I confirmed his statement 10 years later.

"Why do you wanna be a cop, Maggie?" John Tibor sat down beside me in the fire-station kitchen.

I drew a deep breath. It was too complicated and personal to explain. "I'm going to save the world from abuse," I answered defensively.

John Tibor's now familiar smile crossed his face. "Well, that's a good reason, but why would you want to do that?"

"Because I *can't* do it, so it'll be a helluva challenge!"

He walked to the counter, to the large commercial coffee pot. His face became serious, "You know, Maggie, if you ever want to talk, I would be here to listen."

Instead of appreciating his comment, I felt defensive, leery. "I'll keep that in mind, John."

Our conversation was interrupted when Bob Leger pushed the kitchen door open and quickly stepped into the room. Officer Leger had been hired eight months before I was. We had interviewed for this job on the same day. Having the luck of a woman trying to break into this male-dominated profession, I had flunked my first oral interview.

Bob Leger's entrance into the kitchen lightened things up considerably. He was a thin, energetic man who could create a positive electrical force in the air as soon as he appeared. He well-deserved his nickname of "Bones" as he pounded his boney chest with his fist.

"Hey, Maggie, are you ready for the academies?" he asked. "Yee-haa, you should have fun!" And with that, Bob performed some physical gyration that made us all laugh.

Our laughter was short-lived as the familiar clinking of Captain Grant's crutches could be heard coming from the locker room. We looked at each other, and then busied ourselves, trying to avoid any criticism. Nevertheless, I became the target. He focused on me.

"Maggie, did you put those flowers in the bathroom?"

Oh crap! I thought. I had put some floral rubber bathtub stickers on the toilet stall nearest to the wall where the door's gap was less. I was claiming the stall. Then I had put two more on the mirror for a little "feminine" look.

"Yes, I did."

"Don't put anything on State property. I had the graveyard shift take those off." With that he turned and left.

Embarrassed, I quickly left the kitchen area to tend to my assigned truck. I felt I made a mistake—criticizing myself for my ineptness.

Chapter Four

1975

Mom's eyes dampened with tears. "I don't think this is going to be a good trip, Maggie. Are you sure you can't come with me?" She took my hand.

We were in the terminal building. I was still in training and assigned to the fire station, but had received permission from my Watch Commander to join her before she boarded her flight.

I fought my guilt for denying her request and tears welled up in my eyes. "I can't, mom. I would have to start over again in the police academy, and they don't know when they'll have another one. Virginia will be here soon. She'll help you."

Dad had flown to Virginia Mason Hospital in Seattle a few days earlier to check a blood clot in his foot. His lower leg had turned black, and he was scheduled for surgery the next day. The Department had agreed to give me emergency leave to go with my mom to Seattle, but I had made the decision not to go. Virginia would go. Now the headstrong, reliable adult, she was mature beyond her age. I felt good she was going, relieving me of responsibility and guilt.

I embraced my mother as we said goodbye at the indoor boarding gate. I stood motionless as I watched her and my sister board the airplane, worrying if I'd made the right decision. However, the force that pulled me to stay back and finish the academy was so strong I found myself almost in a panic that I might have to leave. I wanted this training; I didn't want to be left behind for *any* reason. This was my direction and I didn't want it interrupted.

Our in-house police academy consisted of 80-hours where we were taught the Alaska State and Federal Laws and Airport Rules and Regulations. I would also be required to pass the weapons proficiency test, which came at the end of the academy. Once out of the academy, the field training or on-the-job training (six months) began.

Four days after mom and Virginia left, was the final day of the police academy, and I was scheduled for weapons qualification. I had never used a pistol and had purchased a used Smith and Wesson .38 caliber, Model 15. Still assigned to the day shift, I had been to the firing range every day after work for two weeks practicing.

I'd been taken under the wing of Sgt. Tenny Malaski who evidently saw in me potential for handling a weapon and donated his time to train me.

"I'll be out there with you when you qualify," said Sergeant Tenny Malaski, in his forties, dark hair, blue eyes, medium build. "So don't get nervous."

Tenny's words were reassuring. He had a lot of patience when it came to training me, and I was thankful for his persistence. His soft demeanor and chuckles eased my tension.

"Do you think I'll do all right?" I asked.

"Maggie, you have good balance. Just remember, balance and breathing, that's what it's all about."

That evening, in my apartment, I placed soup and crackers before me on the table. Another gourmet meal. Cooking for one.

The telephone interrupted my thoughts. Mom and Virginia had been gone three days.

"Hello?"

"Maggie, it's mom."

"Yes? What's going on? How's dad?"

"He just got out of surgery. He's doing fine. Virginia and I are waiting for him to get out of recovery."

I was so relieved. "That's good. How are you doing?"

"Well, you know. I'm still worried. But I'm sure he'll be okay."

I went back to my dinner. The day before when I'd called dad, he'd had the hiccups and said he'd had them for three solid days. We laughed a little and, before I hung up, and for the first time in my life, I told him I loved him. I'm not even sure if I did or how to feel it, but I said it and I'm glad.

I ditched the idea of eating the soup and called my brother, Tiger, to have him meet me at a local restaurant. I was energized by my mom's report.

Tiger had remained in Anchorage following his time in the Coast Guard. He was currently staying at my parents' house until he could find his own place and way. Following a short celebration of food and laughter, we drove to our parents' house where we found our brother, Ben, waiting for us.

Angrily, he demanded, "Where have you been? I've been looking all over for you. Dad died twenty minutes ago!" The message and the tone of delivery were confusing.

It took a few moments for the impact to hit me. Then the anger seeped into the walls of my protected heart as the message of death was delivered so cold and callous.

I was quiet on the following day of work, still trying to work through the shock of my dad's death.

Tenny could sense my uneasiness. "Are you okay?" He raised his eyebrows.

I took a deep breath. "Yes, I'm fine. Just nervous." I smiled weakly, denying my grief.

I had to concentrate. I wanted to finish the academy, and this was the last day. I'd waited for this. I was excited about it. I'd given up seeing my dad for this.

Our weapons firing range was next to the fire training pit on the south side of the airport. The large outdoor range was parallel and adjacent to the east-west runway. The wind often blew there, delivering the noise from jets taking off a half-mile away. It was distracting.

"Just relax, Maggie," Tenny said, "You'll be fine.

The late March air was cool, and snow was still on the ground, but the warmth of the afternoon sun began to strengthen and the blue sky was striking. Spring was around the corner. I shut my eyes and faced the sun. I could hear the chickadees flittering, singing, gliding in the soft breeze.

The Practical Pistol Course (PPC) consisted of shooting sixty rounds at a silhouette target, beginning at fifty yards, then working forward to the seven-yard line, all in a timed sequence. We were required to shoot left and right handed.

Captain Grant, the range officer, yelled, "Go!"

I ran to the fifty-yard line, dropped to the prone position, and drew my gun.

At the end of qualifications that day and all scores were tallied, I placed third in the department with a score of 93 percent among eighty-six officers. I stood next to my target and thought about my dad and how he was no longer in our world. How my life just kept going and his ended.

Over the following months, and years, I was surprised at my own reaction to my father's death. Understanding of his life or his direction or reasons evaded me. It was as though he didn't have a chance to show me a soft side and that his life ended before he could explain it.

But in another sense it was about Alaska: its remoteness and lack of family and friends and warmth and activities and.... Mostly its remoteness made it like a single ice berg floating by itself, severed from the mother—until it melted.

I missed him because there wasn't any other person to miss. He was all there was. No uncles, no aunts, no nephews, nieces, cousins, no grandparents. Nothing. Absolutely no one else except us—the immediate family.

On quiet evenings and early mornings when I worked in the terminal building and for years to come, when the winter darkness helped me focus, I climbed the stairs of the two-story terminal building at the airport, unlocked the observation deck overlooking the runways and airport, and stepped into the night. I visualized the days when he was sober and I could hear him laugh. It echoed among the distant noises of the night.

I always saw him up there, his lean body and curly gray hair. He walked fast leaving us behind. Usually, if he accompanied the rest of the family to the grocery store, he just went his own way. Never waited, never communicated, and we would spend time looking for him. Our time. He had no patience.

Sometimes I saw him with his cigarette between his stained fingers, his ridged nails, as he stood with his hand on his hip, scrutinizing a situation. Although he had no patience, he did seem to think logically before he acted.

He was a self-taught man and it took me years to realize that. Strength and independence had brought him to this country where he'd endured the hardships of a territory that was still as wild as it was unforgiving. He came to the Territory of Alaska during the height of the Depression in the early 1930s.

Thirty years after he died, I found an old newspaper article that gave me a glimpse into the man I didn't know.

The *Press-Scimitar*, Memphis, Tennessee, November 4, 1933: "First to slip away from the family circle was Ben. Too restless to stay in school, Ben shook the dust of Memphis from his feet when he was 22 and headed for the gold country in Alaska."

The article continues: "Taking odd jobs along the route, he worked his way northward. When he reached Alaska, he got a job with the Alaska road commission and in that way reached his goal—the Nebesna Gold Mine, 60 miles from the Arctic Circle."

"'The farther north I went, the tougher it got,'" Ben said this morning. "'It was intensely cold—the thermometer was ranging around 66 below—and the roads had turned into paths.'"

"'Learning from the Indians, I threw away my 'city clothes' and bought some heavy woolens and furs. I wore four pairs of socks under heavy fur-lined moccasins.'"

"With a dog team and a guide, Ben began a 250-mile trek thru the snow and ice, to Nebesna."

"Finally Ben reached the Nebesna mine.

"'It was a sorry looking sight to have traveled 3,000 miles to see,'" he said. "'A few cabins and a lot of tents was all it was—and a hole in the mountain for the mine. But I stayed four years. There must be some fascination, somewhere.'"

"On top of the world, literally, 250 miles from the nearest white settlement, Nebesna Mine was a self-ruled community."

"'There were no written laws in Nebesna,'" Ben resumed, "There were no police—and there was never any trouble. Everyone there worked in the mine.'"

I never knew him. I never understood him. And that was, in part, why I had trouble letting him go. I continued to guess the answers as I walked onto the Observation Deck so many times in the middle of the night.

Even a child whose jaw cracked under the fist of a man who was supposed to protect her— missed him.

Chapter Five

1964

March 27, 1964, 5:36 p.m. Good Friday, Alaska experienced the largest earthquake in North America. Second in the world.

My brother, mom and I were in the living room watching Password when the earth rumbled. We were used to tremors, but this time it was different.

The distant rumbling escalated into a roar. Then a thunder, like a freight train coming right at us.

Mom stood up waving her arms and yelling, "Get out, get out of the house!"

She and my brother, Tiger, made it to the door. I crossed the living room to get my parakeet, Elvis.

Once in the street, it took all my strength to stand. Glass was shattering everywhere and people were screaming. Booms rang in my ears. I desperately hung onto my birdcage.

Four minutes of devastation, 9.2 on the Richter scale. More than 2,000 aftershocks in the first week alone.

The smell of the roast laying on the kitchen floor hit me first when I shoved open the back door. Little was left in the cupboards. Our dinner was on floor, covered in glass and debris. Mom immediately started cleaning up. Then she threw up, not saying anything. No hugs, no explanation, and no wondering if we were okay.

1975

"Management put bets on you saying they could get rid of you in six months."

—Told to me by the Chief's secretary five months after my hire date.

On the way to fire training pits.

One of the most physical and challenging aspects of my career was fighting fires. It takes a great deal of strength, endurance and courage. I didn't take it lightly. The fire academy in March 1975 would either make me or break me. I was 23 years old and my own management placed bets on how fast they would get rid of me. The fire academy just might be their ticket to that end.

The first week consisted of class work. In addition to learning my way around eight very different pieces of apparatus, I had to learn to operate and be tested on them. The class work included the theory of fire fighting, using a variety of fire-suppressant chemicals, operating and maintaining the equipment, identifying every tool on the trucks and its intended use and advanced first aid.

The last rookie left the kitchen after the initial written test, and the twelve of us milled around the truck bays.

"How did you answer number seven?" asked Tom Murrel, a slender built man and one of the few who already had a four-year degree, "the one about what if you..."

"Don't do that!" I said. "I can't stand that. It's over. Don't hash it over now. You'll drive yourself and everyone else crazy."

Captain Edwards, the fire captain, had us gather in the kitchen and handed us our written test scores. Thankfully, everyone had passed.

Then we reviewed the next phase: fighting a live fire. As we sat quietly gathered in the kitchen, I dared to ask a stupid question. "Do you suggest we not eat?"

"No, I don't suggest you *not* eat. Eat lightly. It will be quite a work out."

I squirmed on the radiator among the eleven men. I had been exercising, running, dieting—trying to achieve the necessary strength it would take to fight a fire. I wasn't sure I was there.

I not only did not eat the day before, I didn't sleep either. I was nervous and anxious to see if I could handle this.

The FAA required the airport to conduct live fire-training exercises, which were done yearly. The fire-training area was on the south side of the field, nicknamed "the pits." The fairly large, though shallow, rectangular-shaped pit was bordered on all sides by snow covered gravel berms. It was filled with water about four-inches deep to provide a surface area on which fuel could float; that was one way to save money on fuel and get a fire over a larger area. The below-freezing weather turned the bottom of the pit into an ice-skating rink.

Back then, various airlines were allowed to dispose of contaminated fuel or oils by storing it in 55-gallon drums next to the pit. We then dumped whatever they donated into the pit and ignited it for our training purposes. It was a two-fold situation: the airlines and the airport could readily get rid of their contaminated fuel and oil products and the fire department had a free source of fuel for training.

For the fire training, we positioned two crash trucks adjacent to the pit. One was for safety coverage should anything go wrong. The other was the source of water for the two teams of two who would use the hand lines on the truck.

The two teams entered the pit on foot, side by side, with a supervisor in-between. The supervisor directed the teams using hand signals, because the noise level of the pump engines and our fire fighting hoods precluded hearing verbal commands.

The two teams of two attempted to extinguish the fire by using a fog pattern, sweeping side to side. Because fuel floats on water, the water from our hand-lines merely pushed the fuel and fire away from us. (The water has to cool the fuel before the fire can be extinguished.) Consequently, we ended up chasing the fire around the pit.

There are two purposes for using water for fire training rather then Aqueous Film Fighting Foam (light-water or AFFF) normally used on an actual fuel fire. Water is economical; light-water is very expensive. Also, once you use light-water on a fuel fire, it's nearly impossible to get it to re-light for subsequent firefighters. So, we saved the "real stuff" to be used for the last fire of the last day of training – a grand finale.

Under the early morning darkness and wind-driven snow of early March, our journey to the fire pits began.

"Come on, Maggie. Get into the truck," said another new recruit.

I climbed up into Engine Three and joined the four other officers who were crammed into the cab of the truck designed for three. We piled in the back cab on top of the medical supplies, air packs, forcible entry tools, and fire turn-out gear.

The men helped to ease my tension. I never thought they would be as anxious as I was.

Mike Marshall, a veteran officer, said, "This is going to be nothing. Don't worry about any of this crap. Piece of cake."

A couple of them were seasoned firefighters to assist in the training. I didn't ask any questions, fearing their responses.

The soft green glow within the cab captured the anxiety of one young rookie who dared to ask, "How much fuel do they dump into the pit?"

I glanced toward Marshal, who sat up front and waited for his answer. He hesitated so his words would sink in.

"Oh, probably 400 gallons of contaminated fuel." Mike waited for the effect to hit the rookie.

After having mustered up enough defense, the recruit answered, "Doesn't seem enough to me. Can we go down wind? I'd like an actual challenge here."

His sense of humor lightened our mood as the men chuckled with some reservation. It was like cutting the elasticity of an intensely stretched out rubber band.

Mike, six-foot three, 220 pounds, impressed us with his extensive knowledge of fire fighting. "You'll lose most of your energy in the first twenty seconds." He looked at me. "If you're short, say less than five-nine, you'll be on maximum reserve just fighting the sixty pounds of pressure from the hose." He waited, silently baiting me to fall into his trap.

"Don't worry about me, Marshall," I said. "I lost all my energy just getting into this truck with all the manly clothes I'm wearing. The worst part is, I don't think these silver bunkers go well with the color of my eyes. What do you think?"

I was hoping that would take some wind out of Mike's sails. For a second the whole cab was silent. Then they started to laugh.

The driver turned his head back, "Hey, Maggie might be short, but look at her hair. That adds five inches!" The guys chuckled and I smiled.

We arrived at the pits in three different fire trucks. The snow blew from the west, a reminder of the adverse weather conditions. Our trucks were called crash trucks because we dealt with airplane crashes. The design was much different than those of structural fire trucks like in the cities. Our trucks held large amounts of water because fire hydrants were absent. The small crash truck carried 1,500 gallons of water and 250 gallons of light-water. The larger trucks carried 3,000 gallons of water, 250 gallons of protein foam concentrate, and 250 gallons of light-water concentrate. In 1983, our department obtained a new 6,000-gallon Oshkosh fire truck. It was a Cadillac compared to the old Walters trucks. It rode smooth, fast, and could maneuver off-road. It was a very impressive truck and the largest of its kind in the world.

We left our warm cab and gathered around Captain Edwards for instructions.

I stomped my feet to keep them warm, swaying side to side listening and watching the scene around me. We were like children gathering for story time. Only we didn't know the ending. We were anxious, ready to prove ourselves; yet, for me,

I was scared to death. Not of the fire, but the possibility of my own failure.

Then Captain Edward's voice exploded in my head. "Maggie, you'll be on the back-up hose on the first team going into the pits."

I'm going in FIRST?

Our "proximity suits" were not compatible with wearing an air mask. They were made of an aluminized material, for reflecting the high heat involved in fuel fires. Instead of wearing an air mask with an air tank, (as in a structural fire) we wore a helmet covered by an aluminized cloth-type hood that draped down over our shoulders. A square, plastic face-shield covered with a thin layer of real gold was hinged so we could flip it up to see. No seal. No fresh air. We were forced to inhale the fumes into our lungs—contaminated air, toxic fumes.

We four stood in two teams, Captain Edwards poised between us as our guide. He dumped what seemed like tons of contaminated fuel into the pits then torched it.

The biggest fire I had ever seen grew before my eyes. Black smoke rolled into the air, swallowing the light. Then the flames exploded in hues of yellow, orange, and blue, and immediately absorbed the fuel. As it grew—mesmerizing, beckoning, inviting—the heat penetrated my gloves and prickled like needles on my hands. I pulled my face-shield down. It instantly fogged up. My vision fused in a world of colors and reflections. Nothing was clear. My breathing was intense. *I hope I live through this.*

Captain Edwards yelled over the whining pitch of the pump engines from the trucks. "Let's go!"

The smells of rescue—fuel, sweat, smoke and light-water, soon became familiar to me. Fire and heat. Water, ice. Jubilation. Noise. Camaraderie. I entered a world so foreign to me I questioned my own sanity.

I felt small, insignificant. I stepped up over the three-foot snow berm that encased the fire pit. With the three inches of toilet paper and socks stuffed into my oversized boots, I couldn't feel my way and the downside of the berm did me in. I slid down the hard-packed snow into the pit of fire and ice, and fell hard onto my hands and knees. My fire hood flew off. I searched for it, the intense heat blasting against my unprotected face. I quickly grabbed at the hood. As I pulled it back on the oily smell of fuel spun around the inside of my helmet. I groped for the hose beneath the water and fuel, empty space at each fingertip with oversized gloves made it harder to feel.

My nozzle man opened his hose line. The intense pressure from the spray and the lack of footing pushed us both backwards easily. He turned off the line and on the slick ground we shuffled forward again toward the fire. Although it was my job to guide the nozzle man, I could barely see myself. I pushed him, tapping his shoulder in the direction I felt he should go as I strained to pull and drag the heavy hose behind me. Between the dense smoke and roar of the fiery blaze, I could barely make out Captain Edwards who was guiding the two teams together. I leaned into my nozzle man pushing him towards Edwards. Still, the lack of footing made it a slow and arduous fight to slay the beast.

Then it was over. The sense of thank-god-that's-over comfort followed me as we dragged the hose out of the pit and I sat on the bumper of Engine Five. I took off my hood, my lungs replenishing with cold, pure air as I inhaled deeply away from the dying fumes.

I glanced at Captain Edwards. His usually stiff hair was messed up. I thought he looked better, down-to-earth, and not so sterile. Approachable.

We had a minute to recoup until our positions were switched with our partners. I would be on the nozzle. I was embarrassed about falling so I kept my distance from everyone. I don't think I could even stand the regular bantering at this point. The pressure I put on myself to succeed was enough for the moment.

I couldn't get the hose nozzle into a comfortable position. It was like a machine gun with an inch-and-a-half hard suction hose attached to it. I held onto the three-foot nozzle as the hose draped over my shoulder as I stood waiting for the cue to go in.

Tim Cronin, my back-up, was about 30 pounds heavier than me, a foot taller. He leaned into me over the shrill of the fire engines and said, "It's a bitch, Maggie; lots of pressure and no footing, as you know. I'll stay close behind you; don't worry."

Tim's stature alone gave me some comfort. I figured he could just toss me into the fire if I couldn't get there myself.

More fuel was added to the pit. I put my face-shield down. The combination of heavy breathing, warmth from the fire, cold from the air, and the fact that it was snowing obscured my vision. I was guessing what direction to head. I grasped for footing, inching my way up the berm then slipped. Down on one hand I pushed back up and made it to the other side—into the pit—and into the fire.

The roar of the fire and fire engines was loud and imposing. I struggled with my over-sized bunker gear, trying to wrap my hands around a nozzle that was so antiquated for fire fighting. The design of the hose was cumbersome and not very efficient. I squeezed the handle with everything I had. Nothing. No water. I bent over and leaned on my leg squeezing with my right hand and still, nothing. My frustration swelled.

The fire encircled me and lapped against my legs. The Beast was in control. The fire was touching me - singeing my gear! I yelled to myself: *Maggie, you can do this! Relax. Feel the pressure. Work with the pressure.*

I hated myself. *It's too much! You can't do this! You're weak!*

Captain Edwards moved towards me, "What's wrong?" He yelled.

Then those failing words came out of my mouth, "I can't get it opened."

He took my line and struggled with the nozzle. He finally got the line opened but not without difficulty. He placed his hand around the trigger opening of the nozzle. If he let go, the line would close. I wrapped my hand over his.

"Let go of my hand!" he yelled. "Maggie, let go of my hand!"

I didn't. Frustrated he wiggled his hand out from under mine, leaving his glove in my grip. The line remained open.

My knees bent and I tried to make the side-to-side motion taught in the early training. Muscles I didn't know I had screamed at me. I couldn't understand why I was having so much difficulty since I had practiced many, many times without any problems.

The fire finally died. I let go of my grip on the trigger and the water immediately stopped. My exuberance at not dying was short-lived and premature however. My back-up man tapped me on the shoulder and turned me around. There the fire monster was in all its glory, eating up the unburned fuel behind us.

It taunted, flirted. It would not be conquered. It was in control.

I was exhausted! My reserve was on reserve. I couldn't last much longer.

I squeezed the trigger. It opened, but I wasn't prepared. The pressure threw me backward. Then it turned off.

I tried again. Nothing.

The other nozzle man put out the fire, all of it. I was doomed.

I opened my face mask and took in a deep breath of the winter air, mixed with dying smoke. After we dragged the hose out from the pit. I stood exhausted, a failure.

Captain Edwards came over. "What happened?"

I tried to smile, but was too humiliated. "I don't know. I practiced repeatedly before. Of course, I wasn't in full gear; boots, gloves and bunkers three sizes too big."

"You're wearing bunkers that don't fit?"

"I can barely walk," I responded meekly.

"Well, actually, no one is doing very good. I'm going in there myself with Sergeant Malaski."

I looked up at Captain Edwards. "Well, before you go in, you might want this." I handed him his glove.

He nodded and laughed, "Yeah, why didn't you let go?"

I smiled as he walked away.

Captains Edwards and Sergeant Malaski took their positions as nozzle men, both in good physical shape, with two rookies backing them up.

We lit the fire and stood back.

Captain Edwards took two steps into the pit, leaned forward and opened the nozzle to a straight stream. The pressure from the hose spun him backwards and he fell right on his butt! It was a spectacular fall and probably the angle and pressure from the stream of water hitting the fire created the one and only fireball I'd ever seen. It took everyone by surprise. Laughter could be heard above the pump engines.

Sitting in the fuel and water with the hose pointed straight up, Captain Edwards repeatedly banged on the hose, trying to get it to turn off.

This design of nozzle, if the pressure was too high, would prevent the firefighter from switching from straight stream to fog pattern without turning off the hose completely. Straight stream was unadvisable in the situation of closely encountered fuel fires.

Shuffling through the ignited carbons, the back-up man managed to turn off Captain Evan's nozzle. Without the pressure bearing down on him, Edwards was able to get up then set the disperse pattern on fog. But he couldn't advance into the fire because of all the ice on the ground. After a long, laborious fight with the Beast, they managed to put the fire out.

When Captain Edwards finally came out of the pit, he announced to the mechanic, "Check the truck. There's something wrong with the pressure of this hose. It's way too high."

After a series of checks, the mechanic announced that the hose was pumping 100-pounds per square inch more than normal and he couldn't get it to regulate. He was surprised the engine hadn't burned out.

No wonder I couldn't open the handline. Maybe I hadn't failed after all?

"We'll use Engine Five from now on," said Edwards

Engine Five had handlines designed to pull open. No squeezing 60 pounds of pressure while you fight a fire.

I waited while all the others went through the training pit twice. Edwards then asked for

Maggie (above) during fire training. Taken by Jack Sharp

volunteers to go in a third time. I volunteered. I had to know I could do this.

Before entering the Beast's domain, I watched it grow as it drank the fuel and licked at the sky. With every second that passed, the monstrous fire grew in temperature and intensity, daring anyone to get in its way. I felt a sense of combat as I entered its arena.

There is an eerie silence that surrounds a person when fixed on destroying the enemy and your life becomes at risk. Cops will tell you. And firefighters will tell you. Noise is muffled, almost absent. Focus is sharp.

I lowered myself into a crouched position. Opening the line to show water was a piece of cake. The fire swept dangerously above me as I controlled the water spray that would end its life. For that moment, I was alone, surrounded by a deadly enemy. My senses became one, my breathing labored as the fire circled above me and crackled in defiance. *I can do this!*

With muscles tight and aching, I crouched as low as I could and with my entire weight fought against the pressure of the water hose. Sweat saturated my body as black smoke and orange flames rolled upward, releasing the smell of burnt hydrocarbons. The fusion of sights and muffled sounds, acute awareness and the sense of battle were sharp. The penetrating heat of fire and exhaustion played a game with each other—who would be brave enough to stay in the arena? Who was determined enough to win?

With the ending of one event, another is born. As our team extinguished the fire, and hauled our hose out of the pit, the step of our gait was unmistakable: cocky, arrogant, and confident.

A day of victory.

Fire Academy Anchorage International Airport.
Maggie with co-workers.

Chapter Six

1962

My temples hurt and my stomach was nauseated. My vision was off and my heart was beating faster than normal. I knew I couldn't make the rest of the school day, I was too sick. The school nurse called my mom and asked that she pick me up.

My mom asked, "Can she walk home?"

I weakly nodded to the nurse that I could. I didn't want to upset my mom by having to come get me. And the nurse let me go. I was eleven years old.

I bundled up in my winter clothes and left the school into a cold, wintery afternoon to trek the mile to my house.

I crossed the street near my school in a slow and deliberate walk. The snow was deep or maybe I was just small as I plowed through the off-streets. I knew I was going to be sick so I knelt near a snow bank and threw up. Not wanting anyone to see me, I cleaned my mouth and got up.

Black and white. That is Alaska during the winter, very little color, like my face, drained of energy and happiness and color. The thought of leaving somewhat of a safety net being in school and heading for a home that might not be so safe, made me want to stop. But I was so sick and cold I made myself continue.

Once in my neighborhood, I knew I was going to throw up again so I found a snow pile where the grader piled up the snow and I puked again. This time I laid next to my vomit facing the gray, lifeless skies. I curled my fingers into a fist inside my mittens for more warmth. The little snowballs that clung onto my knitted mittens were splattered with matter.

Then I gave a sigh watching my breath evaporate before me and thought, "Please let me die here."

1975

Captain Grant approached me in the fire stalls where I was checking the essential equipment from my truck. As always he was abrupt and direct, "Maggie, you'll be moving into Costa's locker in the first row. His last day is tomorrow."

As the Alaska Pipeline drew several of our employees onto the icy North Slope, the loss of these officers opened up space in the locker room. This was the main locker room and definitely an upgrade from the chill of concrete and exposure to voyeurism.

Then he turned on his crutches and left. That was it? I stood alone in the truck stalls thinking about my moving into the main locker room. I was excited in the sense it would bring me closer to feeling a part of the department—not so separated. The locker room signified unity. There was a sense of bonding held together by crass jokes, lies, and bragging. Like a team sport—only when I was in high school, women were not allowed to play team sports like men. Now I had an opportunity to learn the dynamics of the team concept as well as have a warm and more private area to dress. I couldn't wait to move into the locker room.

I finished the mandatory check-list of equipment from my truck then walked into the main locker room to see where Costa's locker actually was.

As I faced my to-be locker, twenty feet to my left was the red door to the kitchen and, as with the outer bathroom door, it would remain open. My new locker was strategically located for my maximum exposure. The rows of lockers faced each other, so I would be dressing butt to butt with some guy. To my right, eight more lockers, facing yet another eight lockers.

I was on the corner and all the foot traffic entering or leaving the locker room would pass by me. Those men who had a locker in my row would have to physically squeeze behind me unless I stepped out of my row into the aisle.

At 24 years old, I just wanted to fit in and do my job.

The situation not only offended me; it burst my whole concept of belonging.

I lived in a false expectation of acceptance. *Did I not learn anything from my parents' rejection of me? Did I purposely seek a job that tormented me like my parents? Had I not grown out of the chaos and turmoil? Did I create it?*

Being in the locker room with the men was not the ideal of bonding or being accepted or being equal. It was a disaster that put me on a "meat rack," allowing for further exposure.

I was alone. I was the only woman. The next woman wouldn't start for another month. I could have gone several directions at this point. The anger and frustration in me could have sealed my alienation by voicing my complaints, which I would guess would have made my life worse. Or I could suck it up until my probation period was over and file a discrimination complaint. I chose the latter.

I was dealing with the old "Boys' Club" and don't think for a minute I wanted to be a part of that. The Boys' Club, in my mind, set women back 50 years. But they made the rules and I knew I had to abide by them until I was strong enough to stand completely alone.

I'd been on the job only nine months, three months shy of ending my probationary period, and I wasn't eligible for union representation until I was a permanent employee. If I ever filed discrimination paperwork, I wanted the union to back me.

In spite of the locker room situation, my attitude was kept in check by the police field training, which I enjoyed immensely. My dream was to become a cop – a police officer. The police were the first degree of the "Wheels of Justice." Without their initial suspicion, interrogation, or arrest, the Wheels of Justice did not roll. It was the street cops that initiated justice. I wanted to be a part of that—to make a difference. Like when the police came to our home when the fighting was out of control. There was an aura of safety that radiated from the blue police uniforms like gods of goodness. The protectors. I was willing to sacrifice myself for that goal.

At the time of my field training we didn't have permanent field-training officers or FTOs, so in my "janitor-gray" uniform, I followed each senior officer like a puppy wagging its tail for approval.

One of my favorite assignments was "area patrol." We had two police cars that would patrol the airport property. One was assigned to patrolling Lake Hood and Lake Spenard. The two lakes were interconnected to form the world's largest seaplane base, which housed more than 400 private airplanes. Adjacent to Lake Hood was a gravel airstrip, where another 100 private airplanes were parked. The other patrol vehicle was assigned to patrol everywhere else on the airport, handling everything from traffic enforcement to responding to reported crimes.

Near the end of my first year, I still needed several hours of police training before I could be on my own. The issue of the unfinished training became an everyday irritant for me. Lieutenant Corey went out of his way to mess with me. Older, balding, with a large potbelly and way too many years on the department, he stood next to me at my locker while I was dressing. "You'll be assigned to Engine Four today, not training." He held his clipboard, marking the changes.

The anger of not receiving my training festered inside me like a simmering volcano. I stared straight ahead at my locker, my head spinning in cuss words. I curtly responded, "I don't have much time to finish my training, Lieutenant."

"Can't help you there," he stated in his terse response. Then he walked away.

I waited for Corey to leave the locker room then I stood back from my locker and slammed the door as hard as I could like a two-year-old not getting her way. I couldn't help it. I wanted to hit something or someone—Corey. The walls of the locker room squeezed into my space, choking me; stifling my willingness to stay positive.

I changed into my fire uniform and, without checking out the truck, simply drove it to the East ramp and stayed there until I calmed down.

The deadline for completing my police training came and went. All I needed were three lousy days. The consequences of missing the deadline meant I couldn't go on police duty by myself. Nor would I be able to get off probationary status, which meant a pay raise. Rookies junior to me were getting their training.

I fell into a 'don't-give-a-crap' attitude. I was on remote control, like a robot. I tried not to think of the situation that was eating at me.

Two weeks would go by before Captain Grant finally addressed the situation.

He stood in front of me in the fire station kitchen and barked, "Why aren't you in uniform (meaning the assigned blue police uniform)?"

There were several other officers in the room so I hesitated to say anything but then, with so much frustration, I blurted out, "Lieutenant Corey won't give me the training, sir. I still need three days." I felt like a whiner but couldn't suck it up.

I was surprised at the Captain's reaction. Cursing at the situation, he squeezed his fist in an attempt to control himself. "We'll see about that." He stormed off on his crutches.

My police training resumed the next day and was steady until the last three days were completed. Done. Both police and fire. I surmised that Captain Grant had done what he promised. Completing the training gave me the latitude to be alone in my work. No more holding the hand of a senior officer. I was out of the gray janitor shirt and black pants and into the blue police uniform. I was on my own and I loved it. I had total autonomy. It was like releasing a wild animal that was kept 'under-wraps' for the last year, strapped down in the owner's cage. I was free to make my own decisions. And that was empowering.

Chapter Seven

1976

Most of the men came to work in their civilian clothes and changed in the locker room. I reported in uniform to avoid undressing in front of them. Of course, I couldn't avoid a change of assignment from police into fire and vice versa. Nor could I avoid them dressing next to me.

I successfully finished my probationary period and within two days following my permanent status, I filed a discrimination complaint through the State of Alaska, Department of Labor, regarding the integrated locker room and bathroom. I wanted out of there.

Six days after filing the paperwork, I received notice. I stepped into the kitchen for a cup of coffee after checking my assigned fire truck for the day and noticed new paperwork in my mail slot. The mail slot was a wooden structure bolted to the concrete walls and had some 80 slots where the officers would receive any paperwork.

I anxiously ripped open the envelope.

The official word: "Your complaint of December 4, 1975, was investigated on December 5, 1975. The investigating compliance officer found that there is a restroom that can be locked from the inside at Station #1 and Station #2. Supervisory personnel contacted stated that a change of clothing is not necessary for the job. There were no violations of State Occupational Safety and Health standards noted."

The Chief's bathroom at the front of the fire station was the only secure restroom that locked. The Chief's office was up front near the Alarm Room where everyone punched his time cards in. His bathroom was very small and included a toilet and vanity. It wasn't what I was expecting but I could always change clothes in there as well.

"Whadya reading, Maggie?"

Bob Leger's voice broke through my concentration, and I turned. He was wiping his hands with the rag he used to check the oils on his assigned truck. He walked toward me and I turned back to my official word.

"My results from the State. I'll be using the Chief's bathroom."

Bob reached out. "Let me see that letter." He scanned it, then laughed. "Well, why don't you go see if you *can* use the Chief's bathroom?"

I did and, behold, it was locked. Then each time I asked Captain Grant or other supervisors to unlock it, the standard remark was, "We don't have the key." So, I would give up and go back to the main bathroom and locker room.

The following week Bob Leger approached me. "I've got an idea, Maggie."

I had to be careful of his gleaming, mischievous eyes. He could be convincing.

"Why don't we move your locker to the back area by the Captains' room? Make a little cubby area. Come here and look at it." Bob was lively with his good resolution.

I walked back with him and could see what he was talking about. It would work. If I moved my locker to that area, it would create a barrier between the men and the Captains' office. A little privacy.

Bob and I were both assigned to the day shift and today was Saturday, so the two Captains weren't in. We moved my large locker and created a little separate dressing area for me. I was thrilled!

My regular days off were Monday and Tuesday. When I returned on Wednesday, my little cubby area had disappeared! My locker was back where it used to be. I anticipated punishment. But nothing was said. I continued to push the limits.

Later, standing by my locker I thought of another solution. I turned to Ben Carey, two lockers down.

"Why don't you guys file a complaint about having *me* in here?" I suggested. "Get rid of me."

Ben laughed. "Are you serious? I'll take your perfume over dirty socks any day."

My head went back in disbelief, exasperated. I tried again, "Come on. Someone file a complaint. Any of you!"

Ben went about his business without thinking twice about not filing.

Bob Leger came up and eyed the locker behind me. "I have another idea. Let's take the end locker out. The guys will have to access their lockers without squeezing behind you."

I thought about it. It wouldn't get me out of the locker room, but it might make this misery more acceptable. We took out the end locker, which was empty, and moved it to another location.

The tension in my stomach is always a good indicator of approaching doom. I should have paid attention. I knew I was pushing the envelope. Something wasn't right. Captain Grant hadn't confronted me for the cubby-hole incident and here I was still trying to find a solution for my locker-room situation.

When I came in the next day, the entire row of lockers had been pushed down to fill up the empty space, including the locker behind me. What little protection I'd had was gone. This was even worse! Anger, fear, and confusion erupted.

Then someone behind me yelled, "Maggie!"

The clicking of Captain Grant's crutches filled the air. I didn't turn.

"Don't screw with these lockers! You hear me? You leave them where they are. It is not up to you to make these decisions to change things around. If you touch these lockers again, I'll file a written complaint!"

He clicked away.

I returned a letter to the Department of Labor, Occupational Safety and Health stating the Chief was not allowing me to use the bathroom. And in return, The Department of Labor stated they could not enforce it and it was not a binding decision. Their suggestion was for me to come into work in uniform and leave in uniform. Nothing else could be done.

Chapter Eight

1977

I answered my phone, "Hello?" The wind outside my window whistled in the late December evening.

"Maggie, we've got a 747 over an embankment by Station Two. We're asking for officers to return to work."

"I'll be right there." I hung up without saying goodbye.

All officers within a specific area of the airport were given an emergency home-monitor alarm. When there was an emergency, an alarm would activate the monitor and a certain tone would sound denoting "recall." All off-duty officers would respond back to the airport for the emergency. All other officers were called by the Dispatcher. I lived two miles from the airport and fell within the parameters of the specified "within five miles." However, for whatever reason the department deemed it necessary, I was not privileged to have one of the monitors. I was actually surprised I got any call at all.

Coming out of my apartment, I entered the cold and windy winter evening. It would take a minute for my Valiant to warm up, so I started it, and then ran back upstairs to my apartment to get on some long underwear.

When I arrived at Station One, I checked in with the Dispatcher who was taking names and giving assignments.

"Take a patrol car with Neils." The Dispatcher ordered. "The 747 is just west of Station Two."

"Right."

As I left dispatch, I absorbed the frenzy of activity around the fire station. Even as a second-responder, the excitement of being involved in an emergency charged my entire being. I couldn't wait to get to the scene.

A Japan Air Lines Boeing 747 had been taxiing westbound on the east-west taxiway. Icy conditions and cross winds gusting up to 33 knots caused the jet to slide backwards off the taxiway and sixty feet down an embankment just west of our Fire Station Two parallel to the runway. All 101 passengers and twenty crew members were evacuated safely with only one serious injury. No fire.

As I came over the crest of the hill, the 747 sitting perpendicular in a roadway was so out of place that I found it humorous. "Ron! I can't believe this!" The jumbo jet was lying on its belly across our two-way perimeter road; its bright blue paint stood in stark contrast to the snowy background.

We parked our patrol car on the road just short of the aircraft. Our job was to secure the plane and prevent any people with airport access or the nearby Detox Center from wandering into a secure area.

To get inside the aircraft, we would have to run up the emergency exit chutes wearing our full gear. Standing outside the patrol car with the winds whipping around us, we assessed the situation.

The only way into the aircraft is up the chutes, huh?" I asked Ron.

I suppose so. Come on," he prodded.

Ron was considerably older than I; short but strong. If he was willing...

I held my breath and silently counted, "One, two, three." Then I ran the short distance to the emergency chute. As my boots hit the rubber, I slid backwards on my stomach the entire ten feet. I heard Ron laughing.

I muttered some choice words for him.

"Need some help, Maggie?" a co-worker at the doorway of the chute yelled down.

"Right. Like you're going to come down here to scoop me up? I'll make it."

"Come on," he said. "Piece of cake."

I mumbled, "These chutes were designed for people sliding down not walking up."

Everyone else had made it, so I tried again. I gathered up my body into an erect position, and then stepped up to the chute, one foot after the other.

The bouncing of the chute as I walked on it had the effect of lift-off after every step, like an astronaut bouncing in no-gravity atmosphere.

The co-worker grabbed my hand and pulled me in. "You here for the night, Maggie?"

"Oh, absolutely. What else do I have going on in my life?"

He smiled, and then explained our duties. "Just make sure nothing is messed with. There are a lot of personal items here, purses, and money, whatever. Just leave everything as is for the NTSB. There are four of us assigned inside and two outside. That's about it. Do you have to work tomorrow?"

"No, actually, I'm off. So I'll be here for the night."

The Department's policy was not more than four hours of overtime if you were working, a total of twelve hours; or you could work up to twelve hours at overtime pay on your day off. I lucked out, it was my day off. It was nine days before Christmas so I was glad to get the overtime.

The 747's front landing gear had collapsed and pushed up through the passenger seating. I craned my neck, grateful that the plane hadn't caught fire. The person in the seat that was almost touching the ceiling was the only one seriously injured.

Eventually, the Boeing Company flew an entire crew to Anchorage to fix the 747, which we nicknamed Moby Dick. Its second story hump resembled the whale, thus Moby Dick. Plus it was huge. The crew had removed the wings from the plane for transport to the East Ramp. It took almost a year after they moved the plane from our roadway to the north ramp, to strip it down and rebuild it.

Whenever I was working at the fire station, I drove a truck to the north ramp and watched them work. Like medics in the field, they sewed it back together. No hanger, no warm, dry climate. Just the open air and a few spectators. They worked around the clock, seven days a week. When they were finished rebuilding the aircraft, one of the workers said it was better than when it came off the assembly line. I'm sure it was.

The day it was scheduled to leave our airport, we had our crash trucks on emergency standby. Not because it was a potential emergency. We stood by out of respect, and to say goodbye to Moby Dick. I was assigned to police duties in the terminal building and watched from the observation deck. When Moby Dick roared down runway six-right and the front wheels rotated, I gave silent thanks for their success. Then I left the observation deck

Chapter Nine

1963

I never spent the night with a friend—there weren't any for me so that wasn't an issue. But my brother, Tiger and sister, Virginia, who did have friends, couldn't have them over to spend the night. We didn't want them subjected to our environment; that much we knew. But the day my sister had our neighbor over, who was helping our dad paint the basement, was the day our mom came downstairs to address them. With a gun. She pointed the gun at my sister and said, "I'm going to kill you."

And there were no more friends.

1976

One thing about growing up in an abusive setting is you learn how to keep a secret. Another thing you learn is certain coping mechanisms like denial and minimizing. And having a Plan B or C.

Secrecy is learned from living in an embarrassing household environment: you just don't talk about it. Denial is learned to protect yourself: this isn't happening. And minimizing occurs, for me anyway, down plays the severity of the situation: this isn't so bad, I can deal with it.

The unfortunate reality for me was that I wasn't in control as I thought I would be even once I left the chaos. Instead, without knowing it, I found ways to keep the dysfunction alive. I truly thought once I left home and was free from the tyranny that I could make good decisions. I'd be an adult and on my own and I would be in charge of my life.

I was so wrong about that.

Relationships with men who were close to me were disastrous. Trust was my biggest hurdle; therefore commitment was a huge problem.

Tim Foster was hired eight months before me. He, Bob Leger and I all interviewed the same day. They passed the interview process and I did not. It wasn't until eight months later that I was hired after revisiting the whole application process.

Initially, Officer Foster ignored me. Then, occasionally, he got off a derogatory remark, especially when passing me in the locker room. It was in jest and I suppose flattering in a male-oriented way. He couldn't let his guard down around all the macho men. *Oh, so you like the girl?*

When I first looked up to his 6'0, (me 5'6") his blond hair was striking against the blue police uniform and navy Stetson hat. His eyebrows were so blond; they disappeared into his fair skin, setting off his bright blue eyes and killer smile. He was good looking.

Tim had a stable background, although I felt his career-military father was stiff and uncompromising. Tim's mother was warm and giving, although she too had high expectations. Both our roots were middle-class.

We began seeing each other some 18 months after my hire date. It was a quiet relationship. We didn't even acknowledge each other at work—like living in two different worlds. It was hard to see each other; rotating shifts meant it was hit and miss whether we worked together, plus we had different days off. Also, Tim was in the Air National Guard and I was in the Army National Guard, which consumed our regular days off once a month.

It was a tricky relationship and by no means easy. First my whole chaotic background prevented me from trusting so I was often flippant about the relationship, not compromising, pushing any limits I thought would discourage Tim. *Find someone else, I'm not worth it.*

Second, of course was the whole working relationship.

Tim stood tall behind the kitchen counter as I entered, swinging open the kitchen door to the fire station. We were working the same shift. He was alone in the kitchen.

Tim blurted out, "Why don't you quit this job and marry me?" It seemed he wasn't even prepared to say that himself.

No work-up, no "Hello I love you"—he just blurted it out as I walked through the door.

I was quick and to the point in my response as I laughed out loud. "It took me more than a year to get this job. Why don't you quit?"

I'm sure he was not expecting that, as he stood still not responding.

I was only thinking of my own position as a woman. I was small town, fighting my own personal demons and issues. I had a job that paid men's wages and I not only loved the pay check but the job itself. At this point in my life I wasn't going to give this up for anyone or any reason.

"Nepotism in the business world, nepotism is the practice of showing favoritism toward one's family members or friends in economic or employment terms." www.encyclopedia.com.

The State had strict nepotism rules. Relatives could not work together (married couples, first relations, etc.) Quite simply, we couldn't get married because we both worked at the same job.

In May of 1976, in spite all my reservations, I accepted Tim's proposal—but I refused to quit my job. So, I filed my first nepotism waiver with the State of Alaska to get married. The waiver was quickly denied for the following reasons: (1) Neither of us would be promoted (2) Our attention would alter during an emergency and (3) We could never work the same shift.

Any hope of marrying Tim was on hold. I moved in with him.

When I told mom I was moving in with a man, she yelled at me at the check-out counter in the middle of a grocery store. "How can you do that to *me*? It's not right!" Then she started to cry.

The Department's perception of my living with Tim supported mom's point of view, negating certain requests: some officers ask for special consideration to be assigned the same days off as their hunting or fishing buddies, or other reasons. Usually, the switch was made to accommodate them. All it took was a memo stating they wanted certain days off. They didn't have to put down a reason.

So, I submitted a memo to Captain Grant, requesting the same days off as Tim Foster.

One day while working Dispatch, I flipped the intercom into the alarm room and heard, Captain Grant having a conversation with a lieutenant—discussing my request for days off with Tim.

"If Foster has Tuesday and Wednesday off, then Holeman will never get them!"

Request denied.

****

A normal rotation into the fire station usually occurred every 28 days. However, often people called in sick and changes of assignments were always to be expected upon arrival on duty. I always enjoyed the fire duties and it was a good break away from thousands of people around me on a daily basis in the terminal building. Working fire duties did have its particulars like hours of routine busy-work, occasionally interrupted by terror.

Not only did we work police and fire, but we also rotated and were trained on dispatching. When my duties were completed in the fire station, I usually helped out in Dispatch.

I stepped into the small separate building adjacent to our fire station where George Coffin, who was in his 50s, sat at the main console table listening to the aircraft traffic as well as the police chatter.

"Hi, George," I said as I sat in a swivel chair at the second radio console with my dinner teetered on my lap.

"What's going on, Maggie?"

"Nothing. Thought I could eat up here and help you out if you want."

George Coffin was very meticulous about his dispatching and always backed up his type-written log with carbon paper. I knew he didn't need my help.

"Sure, I could use the bathroom," and he slipped out of Dispatch.

The warmth from the plate felt good in the drafty Dispatch office. The lone space heater had been cranked up as far as it would go but the January cold was encroaching. With only five hours of day light in January, it was dark when I began work at 4 p.m. The soft lighting helped keep down the reflection from the large windows and away from the dark, foggy evening. At just before 6:00 p.m., I had a whole night ahead of me.

I realized George had been gone for about 15 minutes as I flipped the intercom to the kitchen.

"Hey, Coffin, you back there?"

I could hear the rustling of movement then his voice, "Yeah, what's up?"

"What's up is you are working Dispatch and I'm on a truck. I'm wondering if you forgot about me or you're still on the toilet."

"Yeah, yeah, I'm coming up." I visualized his smile as he made a comment to the other fireman in the kitchen, Bob Leger. Bob and George could be quite the pranksters but I couldn't quite make out what he said.

George entered the Dispatch building and sat down.

"Did you miss me?"

"Not in the least," I said as I finished up my dinner.

Then the crash phone rang. It had been two weeks since the Moby Dick incident.

Immediately, I set my plate on the console and stood up while I read what the Dispatcher was writing. Coffin hit the all-call button that alerts the entire fire station and dispatched the trucks.

"Attention in the station, attention in the station. We have a possible Lear jet down at the approach end to runway Six-Left. Eight souls on board, no hazardous materials; all units respond."

I quickly left Dispatch with the alarm blaring and echoing against the concrete walls of the fire station, stepped into my bunker gear, (which finally fit after Capt. Edwards ordered them), pulled up the bunker pants and suspenders, and hoisted myself into Engine 3.

As the stall doors raised to the full open position, I pushed the foot pedal down causing the massive diesel engine to lurch forward. All 60,000 pounds of her. I hit the siren and was aware of the station sergeant in Engine 5 and Bob Leger next to me in Engine 2. All moving as a team. All on the same page.

I was surrounded by the smells of rescue: diesel fuel, light-water, and exhaust as I pulled out of the stall; soon I would smell the blood, the jet fuel and death. This was my first crash with fatalities.

Eight people onboard. Six dead. Ran out of fuel. No fire. Visibility a quarter of a mile or less; ceiling 300 feet. Freezing rain and an eight degree temperature. Hit short of the runway. January 3, 1976. Saturday 5:58 p.m.

The Lear was a small, executive twin turbojet aircraft and was usually chartered for special occasions. This aircraft was coming in from Deadhorse near Prudhoe Bay pipeline camp and was transporting oil officials to Anchorage.

So quickly it happened. First they were on final approach to landing, and then there was silence, nothing. An emergency locator beacon was picked up by a Boeing 747 who was taxiing. According to Homer Powers of the NTSB (news article *Anchorage Daily News*, January 5, 1976) "... the plane apparently hit a rise on line with Runway 6 Left short of the paved surface. Evidence indicated the plane bounced twice, coming to rest in a big gully between the runway and the taxiway."

The debris was spread out as the Lear bounced, hitting the earth, severing part of its landing gear then larger pieces before it came to a halt almost a mile from impact. The plane was upside down and the fuselage was largely intact.

There was no fire. As I approached the crash site and remained in my truck waiting for instructions, I took in the scene: the twisted metal obscured by the fog, an airplane destroyed only moments before, and violent death. The landscape was black and white, the terrain uneven. Diesel fumes from my truck silently crept into the cab. It was cold but my adrenalin kept the chill at bay. I was about to see something I'd never seen before: dead bodies.

I wasn't involved in the rescue of the two survivors but was responsible for helping bag the remaining bodies. Getting out of my truck, I was partnered up with Bob Leger.

Bob Leger's ability to cope with the unpleasantness came in his black humor as he helped me pick up the bodies and place them in the body bags. One man's legs were going the wrong way. "At least he died with his boots on," he said.

I picked up the feet while Bob picked up the shoulders of the man with boots on. As we lifted the body of a stranger, the winter chill not only touched my face, but my soul. The loss of life so instant, so immediate and final. Just a moment ago they were in a warm cabin of an executive jet, then suddenly and violently spilled onto the snowy earth in pieces. I questioned who was I to be the one to touch their bodies, to put them in body bags and seal them up into the darkness of death. One thing I would learn to appreciate was my ability to deny, minimizes, and not let my mind wander. As a child, I developed those coping mechanisms to save myself but in rescue, it enabled me to do my job.

After getting off shift at midnight I drove home to my small apartment. Even though it was Saturday night, there was little traffic within the short distance of seven miles I had to drive home.

I walked up to my second story apartment and turned the key to door #25. As I walked in, I threw off my coat and opened the refrigerator and pulled out a beer. It went down fast and easy so I opened another and sat there alone thinking about the evening. Then I drank another.

Finally, I drifted into numbness.

Chapter Ten

1976

My hand came across my chest as I reached for the alarm clock. Five-thirty in the morning.

I rolled over and hit the alarm. "Too early," I said out loud to no one. Because no one else lived there.

I lay on my back and rubbed my eyes. I knew if I didn't get up immediately, I would simply fall back to sleep, so I hopped out.

The two-room efficiency apartment was cool in the morning. Although I didn't have to pay for heat along with the rent, I found the coolness at night easier to sleep in.

I rolled out of bed in my man's cotton white t-shirt and electric blue hi-leg silk panties. Coming around the corner to the bathroom I used the facilities then walked into the living area. I pulled back the green vinyl curtains that overlooked the parking lot from the second-story to see the weather. It was still so dark only the lighted street lamp gave me any indication of today's weather. Cold. The crystal sparkles of snow crust told me the day was clear of clouds.

"At least it's not a snow storm like the first day of work," again saying out loud to no one.

I got dressed in sweats, did a few stretches, and then headed outside with a light coat. I ran the two-mile stretch alongside Jewel Lake Road between my apartment and Dimond Blvd. and back. Often times, I would see an Anchorage Police car drive by me, waving. Not too many people were out that early and I found peace in the dark, cold air running alone, watching my breath bounce in front of me.

Back at my apartment, I punched the button to the night-before-set-up-coffee then turned on the radio to hear the news.

When the coffee was done, I poured myself a cup of black gold and headed for the shower. The cup sat insecurely on a small ledge inside the shower away from the main cascade of water. I would drink the whole cup before I got out of the shower.

My hair took the most time in my morning ritual. I had to dry it with a towel then I rolled my curls into heated curlers to straighten them. It was a fruitless endeavor since any humidity that made contact with my curls would frizz them out. But, I was determined to straighten my hair if only for the morning drive to work.

I dressed in my fire station uniform, put on a little make-up then searched the refrigerator for breakfast. I'd never been a big breakfast eater. A piece of fruit was about all I could handle until about 10 a.m. then I would be starving. I packed my lunch for the day and grabbed my keys.

Without putting my coat on, I went outside, down the stairs to start my car. Then I ran upstairs to wait for my car to warm up in the 12 degrees above zero cold. It was six-fifty in the morning and I would be at work at least thirty minutes early – as I would do for the remainder of my career.

At 7:15 a.m. I arrived at the fire station. The station was located in a secure area on the east apron of the airport. The employees could park to the side of the station so parking was never an issue.

I entered the fire station through the door that entered the stalls on the west end. This part I would remember vividly and forever. Like the details of fighting my first fire during the academy. Only this vision was reinforced day after day after day.

I knew how lucky I was to have this job. And I knew I would have to continuously earn it to keep it. I'd been on the department 18 months and had worked three major airplane crashes and a multitude of police responses. But this part, walking through the stalls every morning or afternoon or evening when I came to work I would remember the most.

It was the smells. The soapy light-water—a retardant substance that smothers the fire by taking its oxygen. Like bubbles in Dawn soap. Only this "soap" is so powerful that when I reached into the concentrate bare-handed I saw that it immediately stripped me of my nail polish.

The nauseating protein foam mixture—made of ground up animal blood and guts that is designed to stick on the side of a fuselage to smother the fuel fire.

The diesel—the smell of big engines and loud idles.

The oils—permeating in the fire station stalls.

The visual of the fire trucks—red, demanding, imposing. A machine that could plow through anything at any time to rescue you.

The tools—maintenance tools and cleaning tools that neatly hung from rubber holders that were screwed into the concrete.

The concrete—the grey, cold hard siding that stared us in the face every time you walked into the stalls. And the concrete flooring—only separated across the bays in the center by a small drain that sucked in the debris and, on occasion, the blood from death.

The red and white checkered stall doors.

The bunkers that lay on the floor at each driver's door. Each respondent willing to risk his lives to protect an unknown.

There was a sense of connection.

Of pride.

Of unity

I leaned against the counter in the Alarm Room facing the Station Sergeant. The time clock was behind me. I didn't have to wait long to punch in. Only a few men came in this early. I chatted with the off-coming mid-shift station sergeant for a minute before I checked in then headed for the locker room.

Most of the mid-shift was in the kitchen. After I took my bunkers to Engine Two I walked into the kitchen to find Dale whom I was relieving on the truck.

"Hi, Dale," I said, watching him across the large kitchen area.

Dale said, "Hey, you got Engine Two?"

"Yep, my bunkers are by the truck. Anything going on with it?"

Dale came across the kitchen, "Let's walk out here," he said as he moved me toward the kitchen door.

"You need to do a P.M. today (Pre-maintenance check).

"Are you serious?" I said with a hint of irritation. That would take almost four hours to complete. It was a detailed overall maintenance check of the vehicle.

"Yeah," he started, "but that's not all. You have a small air leak on the brakes. Takes forever to get the truck going. We called the Shop but no one there on the midnight shift to fix it."

I had the *Oh Gee, anything else?* look on my face but didn't say anything as I faced Dale.

He got it. "No, that's it. Really, no big deal. Have a great day." Then he slapped me on the back and walked away.

I walked back to my locker to get the rest of my bunker gear when Lt. Corey came up to me. He stood to the side of me with his clipboard. His bald head and pot belly edging into my space.

Having the Watch Commander address me in the locker room meant one thing to me: change of assignments.

"What is it, Lt. Corey?" I asked not looking at him.

"Well, it looks like you'll be working in the terminal building, 602 (Lower level of the terminal building)."

I was so seldom assigned to the fire station that this change pissed me off. The only thing that tempered my disposition was that I wouldn't have to perform the P.M. on Engine Two.

I waited for Corey to leave so I could change my clothes. He stood there without saying anything—feeding my contempt.

Still focused on my locker in front of me, I barely mustered enough of a response without being insubordinate. I flatly stated, "I need to change."

He turned, mumbled something and left.

I wanted to physically strike out and rip his face off.

In the Terminal Building, John Tibor worked the upper level, while I worked the lower. The uneventful evening was broken by a call from a Loomis Security employee who was checking bags in the Western Airlines baggage area. More than a hundred passengers had just debarked and were picking up their luggage.

"602 (call-sign for the person working the first floor of the two-level terminal building) contact Loomis Security in the Western baggage area regarding possible man with a gun."

I was upstairs at the time of the call and quickly made my way down. The escalator brought me directly next to the Western baggage area. As I stepped off the escalator, I contacted Suke, the security agent.

"That's him over there, Maggie." She pointed to a phone booth ten yards from where we stood. "He came down here, got his luggage, opened it up, and pulled out a gun. Then he loaded it and put it in his belt, or somewhere under his coat." Suke was shaking. "Be careful, Maggie."

"Okay, Suke, thanks. I'll be fine." As we talked, I never took my eyes off the man by the phone booth. I knew backup was on its way but right then, I was the only one there.

"Who's that other guy coming toward us, Suke?" I now focused on another young gentleman, about the same age as the suspect. He was walking alone in our direction. It was a wild guess on my part, but I felt the two men might be connected.

"I don't know, Maggie."

Curious about who this other man was, I took a million-in-one chance. Keeping my attention on the man at the phone booth, I approached the other man and grabbed his arm. "Is it you or your buddy that has a gun?" I said.

He spread his arms away from his body. He was wearing a blazer and, when he lifted his arms, a shoulder-holster was exposed. It held a semi-automatic pistol.

I immediately moved him to the wall, and began searching him. I had my back to the first suspect by the phones. Bad situation. I radioed again for backup.

John Tibor arrived shortly after and stood behind me.

"John, the guy behind us has a gun, too. The one by the phone booth."

While John kept an eye on the other suspect, I reached inside this young man's blazer, removed his weapon, and handed it to John. I continued searching the guy, then cuffed him, and placed him under arrest for carrying a concealed weapon.

John approached the other suspect and I followed with my prisoner. A third officer finally arrived, and he and John questioned the other man, searched him, retrieved another semi-automatic, and placed him under arrest as well. The subsequent interview of the two men disclosed that they felt they "needed to protect themselves" and therefore, had felt it necessary to carry weapons.

Chapter Eleven

1961

I believe the reason my parents gave me a dog was that they thought I needed something to connect to. The dog would be a substitution for a missing link in my emotional makeup. A dog would make me healthy. A quick fix, like an ice cream cone. Even my parents didn't know it was *them* and the atmosphere they created that was making me sick.

I spent seven years of my childhood in and out of sporadic episodes of sickness due to the abusive and violent atmosphere of our home. I trailed in and out of hospitals, surgeries, and doctor's offices for all of them to guess my condition.

The puppy, which I eagerly named Nebesna, was four weeks old and brought a connection to me that relieved all other stressors. I'll never forget. He had short hair with floppy ears: bronze and black features with feet he would have to grow into. I loved his puppy smell, his tail wagging ferociously and eagerness to please. The way he licked my face with his little pink tongue as his whole body moved with excitement and the expectations of safety and happiness. The puppy and the daily routine it took to care for him brought a sense of unconditional love that I had never experienced. Even at age ten, I re-directed my focus from self-preservation to that of the dog's welfare. My parents were right—it gave me a new positive direction. But only short-lived.

One night I let him outside to go pee and then I couldn't find him. He had been with me only two weeks.

Shortly after Nebesna disappeared, my parents sent me to Virginia Mason Hospital in Seattle for extensive testing to see what was making me so sick all the time. My dad flew down with me then left me with cousins and an aunt and uncle I had never met.

At Virginia Mason the nurses were so good to me that I felt free. I felt safe. So naturally—I felt well. They pumped my stomach, did brain scans and poked me with needles.

I flew back alone.

Some days after I got home from Seattle, I was doing the dishes in our kitchen. My mom came into the back door where it opened behind me as I stood facing the far wall with two stainless steel sinks, washing dishes.

Without regard to a ten-year old in any sense, she stated, "Virginia Mason Hospital just reported to us you are "psychosomatic" and you create your own illness."

With her hand still on the door bringing light into the small kitchen, her demeanor was tense and that of anger and disgust as she added, "You just cost this family $5,000, too, for Virginia Mason Hospital to tell us you are sick in the head!"

I froze facing the wall as her words burned into my memory, trying not to cry. No more tears. Disassociate.

Nebesna was never found.

1977

DC-8 crash. Unknown photographer.

"Maggie, don't come in here," Sergeant Siegmann insisted. "You really don't need to see this."

I moved him aside as he attempted to block my entrance to the fire-station stall. The sight of the five opened body bags lying on the floor seared a gruesome image into my memory. A lifetime of shelving pictures, tucking them into the back of my mind, trying to suppress what I was seeing. Still I remember them. And the smell of death. These were once men—walking, talking, and living. Now they lay in body bags, mutilated. Some missing half their heads, their brains exposed; eyeballs dangling from what were once their sockets. Blood-soaked clothing ripped and shredded as though a monster grabbed, then tossed them into the air like string puppets. They lay heavy under their lifeless mass—their substance gone.

The stark reality of death staring me in the face. I had never seen anything like this before. And when I walked out, I hoped I would never see anything like it again.

In the early cold morning fog, we approached the bulk of the disaster. Sitting in the passenger seat of the patrol car, I tried to comprehend the scene before and all around me: north, south, east, and west. Fifty-six cattle, all dead. I watched smoke rise from the bodies.

All five crew members died. There was no one to rescue. As I rolled down the window to get a better look, the stench of burning flesh invaded my senses and the putrid, sickening smell mixed with jet fuel filled the inside of the patrol car, making me immediately turn up the windows.

Our job was to secure the scene for an investigation. The DC-8 jetliner had crashed only seconds after take-off at 6:35 a.m. on this foggy Thursday morning, January 13, 1977. It had failed to maintain sufficient speed and climbed only one-hundred feet before losing altitude and veering to the left. It struck the ground at more than 100 miles per hour just off the runway and released fuel that instantly ignited, scorching the snow-covered earth. The debris field covered three-thousand feet in length. The remains of the fuselage lay on a knoll off the west end of the runway. It had disintegrated upon impact.

I stood in silence, gripped by the thought less than two hours ago the men on this plane were alive and now I was only looking at a cold, metal tomb. I diverted my eyes as watched my breath float in front of my face in the 14 degree air.

I joined the first response crew to receive my instructions. They had extinguished the initial fire, which stretched over a large debris field.

We stepped over luggage, personal items and metal wreckage, and skirting around the cattle all shrouded in fog. It was an eerie and bazaar sight. The National Transportation Safety Board (NTSB) agents were working to piece the puzzle together. How could they filter out the deaths? I wished I could. Instead, my mind soaked in the foreign sight.

I reported to Sergeant Malaski for instructions. I was told to take the hand lines from Engine Four and put out any remaining spot fires. I would be relieving the driver of Engine Four that was on scene.

"What are they going to do with all the cattle?" I asked Sergeant Malaski, while hoisting my hose line.

"Donate them to the poor. With the weather so cool, we have some time. Right now," he continued, "just watch for hot spots. When you're done, take the patrol car and pick up the stretchers at Station Two. Take them to Station One and rinse them off. Then re-service the returning trucks."

I acknowledged his instructions and looked back at the devastating scene.

"Did you bring the hamburger buns?" A firefighter joked to another, referring to the cattle.

I was disgusted, listening to their distant conversation. But I laughed, to ease my tension and mask the surreal sight.

Intense lights powered by generators split the early fog like ghostly fingers, and beyond that: darkness. We would have to wait for the late winter sun to rise to see the whole picture.

The darkness and fog protected my senses from overload, the ungodly sight processing in small bits. Then the sun rose over the mountains and the shroud lifted, forcing me to absorb the devastation.

Having extinguished all the spot fires in my area, I was relieved of my engine and took the patrol car to Fire Station Two as directed. My mind drifted. This was my second airplane crash with fatalities. The only dead body I had seen before being employed was my father at his funeral. He had been neatly dressed and sewn together.

My ability to cope, detach and deny came easily to me since I was raised in an alcoholic environment—violence one day, silence the next, no apologies, no reason, and no explanation. No sense.

"Debriefing" and "Crisis Intervention" didn't exist yet. One merely adapted and chose her own path for salvation.

I easily slipped into callousness and lived on the surface of my feelings. The drive to serve and protect and rescue was top shelf and it overshadowed any need to be rescued myself.

In later years, a New York City firefighter, who was working during the 911 terrorist attacks, told me after I retired, "If you're afraid to die, then you're afraid to live."

Why we tiptoed on the edge of death is a question all rescue people ask themselves. Back then; a world outside sirens, red lights, and adrenaline was inconceivable to me. Without it, I would have to look inside… and I wasn't ready.

The price I paid was having to face danger without being rescued myself. This world sucked my emotions into a darkened abyss as I foolishly denied my own vulnerability. I wasn't brave enough to look deep. Beyond the surface.

This is the world of rescue people. We walk alone. We carry the memories. Sights, sounds, smells. The turbulent sleep.

I was out to save the world. But who would save *me*?

Back at Station One, I unloaded the canvass stretchers from the patrol car and hauled them into the truck stalls where an open trough water drain was covered by metal grates. I grabbed a garden hose off the wall and rinsed the canvas stretchers. Snow and blood dissolved down the drain.

I wasn't prepared for the amount of blood that washed into the drains. There was no such thing as the proper handling of biohazards back then. The gore from the canvas stretcher slowly seeped into the unknown as I wondered whose remains were being carried beneath the floor of our fire station.

And would I sleep tonight?

Chapter Twelve

1962

When my dad pushed all three of us kids outside onto the porch then locked the door to our entry, I thought it was fun. We were all in pajamas, no shoes and it was about 10 degrees above zero outside. We had fun for about five seconds.

Then we were cold and we were young and the door to our safety was locked. Age 12, 11 and 10.

"You go in first," Virginia and I were saying to our brother, Tiger. He was the "Lamb of God," whatever that meant. Tiger was our mom's favorite and she had declared that name to him.

Tiger was short for his age and stout. Not fat; strong. He got his nickname, Tiger, when he was born too small and frail, about five pounds. Dad gave him the nickname in hopes to give him a boost through life.

He had a kind heart, too. He was the mediator – the compromiser. He hated the violence; he tried everything to keep the peace. He had black, curly hair and small, dark eyes that twinkled when he laughed. Tiger was one year older than me.

The frigid air hugged us as we stomped our feet to help our circulation, jumping up and down on the porch next to the door that would keep us alive. We were screaming to our father to let us in.

Nothing.

We banged on the door.

Nothing.

We pushed our brother forward and banged on the door again. Rang the doorbell about twenty times.

Finally, the door opened. Dad stood there in his drunkenness not moving.

Until my sister and I pushed the Lamb of God into the doorway. Then my dad's fist struck Tiger and he went down.

My sister and I stepped over Tiger saying, "Thank you, Lamb of God for your sacrifice."

Then we rushed to hide elsewhere.

1977

In 1977, our little city-within-a-city was more than 4,500 acres in size with a population of more than 3,000 employees. On any given day, the Anchorage airport would see over 400 landings and takeoffs, 6,000 passengers checking in or out and 850,000 pounds of jet fuel being pumped.

Because Anchorage International Airport was the Cross-Roads of the World, we had dignitaries, celebrities and politicians who touched our land for a moment or a day. And we, as airport police, provided security on such welcomed visitors. I remember Pope Paul II, Paul McCartney, Sandra Day O'Connor, President Jimmy Carter's son, Princess Diana's parents and the Emperor of Japan, Hirohito. There were many other movie celebrities but I guess the one I remember most—who was not a celebrity in Hollywood sense, but a celebrity in my eyes—was Sandra Day O'Connor, who was the first woman Supreme Court Justice of the United States.

I left the Alarm Room after punching my time-card. I was assigned to Engine Three on the day shift. I entered the dressing room to change for duty and was fumbling around with my combination lock when I got a sense of more than normal officers were in the locker room. They seem to be skirting around rather close by.

The lockers were large, about two-and-a-half-feet wide by six-feet high, with an area for hangers on the left and shelves on the right.

Finally I opened my locker and was reaching to unzip my coat to take it off when I screamed!

There Kenny Mitchell was crammed into the left side of my locker, so contorted he could barely say, "Boo!" His left arm was wrapped above his head, his legs bent at the knees, which were shoved up against the inside of the locker. He couldn't move. The guys must have had to place him into the locker. He couldn't get out by himself.

I could hear the guys laughing, then coming up to see the sight.

"Kenny!" I said starting to laugh myself. "You scared the crap out of me!"

Kenny squeaked a small message, "Can you help me outta here?"

"I don't think so, buddy," then I slammed the door and turned the combination lock. "Good thing you're short, Kenny, I don't know how else you could fit in there!" *How did he even get inside my locker with my combination lock?*

I heard him yelling. The guys were still laughing, telling me to keep him in there. They weren't expecting that I would do that.

"I'm gonna fart in here!" Kenny yelled.

Okay, I thought, I better get him out.

As I opened the locker, I said, "Okay, okay, just don't stink up my locker." I pried him out.

The roll call buzzer sounded and I sat in my favorite spot in the kitchen—either by or on the radiator. The radiator was big—three people could sit on it and I liked my back up against the window.

Following roll-call, I took the check list for Engine Three and completed the daily task. Dale Falk was working with me in the fire station. He was assigned to Engine Four.

I swung open the fire station door that lead into the Alarm Room, then stepped to my immediate right and opened the Alarm Room door to the outside. I walked the twelve steps it took me to get to the Dispatch building.

"Hi, George, what's up? Need any help?"

George swung the swivel chair around to face me. "Did you get Kenny out of your locker, Maggie?" Coffin laughed. I knew he had the intercom opened so he could hear everything.

"Yeah. Was that your idea, George?"

No response, just a smirk.

"I could use the company up here. Nothing going on right now."

Maggie in Dispatch

I settled in the second console and was watching the airport activity on the ramp when the phone rang and I answered it. It was from an off-duty firefighter.

"Hey, did you hear about an airplane crashing near Jewel Lake Road?" His voice was anxious.

"No, I didn't hear anything." I looked at George, "Hey, George, are you getting any calls about an airplane crashing near Jewel Lake?"

"No, nothing."

"Okay, I said to the off-duty officer, "We'll monitor it."

No sooner than I said that calls started coming in from more off-duty firefighters.

A plane had crashed into a house located in the sub-urbs of Anchorage off Jewel Lake Road near the Anchorage International Airport. As I intently listened to information being relayed, I called Captain Edwards over the intercom.

"Has the City asked for us?" he said.

I turned to the dispatcher for an answer. "No."

Edwards immediately called the Anchorage Municipal Fire Department. Yes, due to the aviation fuel spillage, they very much needed our help. We carried light-water and protein foam that would suppress a fuel fire, something the city fire department didn't have. Knowing I would be responding in a major piece of fire fighting equipment, I anxiously waited for our captain to dispatch the call – the call for mutual aid.

It was January 31, 1977—only two weeks after a DC-8 slammed into the runway at Anchorage International Airport just seconds after take-off killing all five crew members and fifty-six head of cattle.

The antique twin-prop Chase YC-122 had just taken off to the south, then dropped and crashed three miles from the airport. There were three people on board. The house was empty. No fire.

Captain Edwards arrived in the Dispatch office and turned to me.

"Take Engine Three."

I turned to leave, the sweat already in a warm glow beneath my uniform before Capt. Edwards was even called. I was going to have to do this by myself.

He grabbed my arm. "Maggie, take Dale with you."

Engine Three was a crash truck. Crash trucks, unlike the city fire trucks, were designed to be driven and operated by one person. Water could be dispersed from a large overhead hydraulic turret controlled by one firefighter from inside. However, if we used hand lines from the truck, more personnel were needed; one person would operate the pump engine while the other dragged the hand line to the scene. Good to take two people.

The alarm's shrill whistle cut through the station and the noise of the chain clanging through the rungs of the rising stall door made my pulse race. I dashed out of Dispatch and rushed to the truck, kicked off my boots and stepped into my fire gear. At 26, I had three years on the Airport Police and Fire Department and this was my fourth airplane crash.

Dale, five years younger and ten pounds heavier than my own 140-pounds, grabbed the rail and swung up into the driver's seat. I slammed the passenger door as we pulled out of the stall with red lights flashing and the siren blaring. Although I was assigned to this truck, I let Dale drive because, as a passenger, I would draw the hand line—and that's where I wanted to be. In the mix. Front line.

Our large crash truck, carrying 3,000 gallons of water and 500 gallons of lightwater and protein foam, had a lot of traction on the packed snow as Dale expertly maneuvered down the two-lane road for three miles to the crash site. It wasn't often we left airport property.

As we approached we saw the airplane's tail section protruding from the remnants of the home that had been leveled. No occupants had been inside the house; however, there were three crew members onboard the YC-122.

We couldn't get near the site. There were too many City fire trucks and police cars were in the way. Dale laid on the air horn and finally, the chaos parted.

After jockeying through the vehicles, Dale got close enough for me to pull out the hand line. The potential for fire was phenomenal. I used the hand line, spraying lightwater to completely cover the aircraft and prevent the pooling fuel from igniting. After several minutes of spraying, I remained on standby with the hose. In case the whole site should explode. A shiver crept up my spine. What would be the point? If the plane exploded, I would go with it.

I halted a man who held a meter and asked, "Can you tell me what you're doing?"

"Trying to get a reading on the natural gas leakage. It's everywhere."

Aviation fuel, natural gas, electricity. Boom!

To overstate the life threatening danger of that day would be impossible. The explosive situation had my mind floating in a world other than reality. Death—my own. Was this my day? How close was I to it for merely being on the scene? Involuntarily, my mind visualized the violent detonation of exploding fire with metal debris and the feeling of intense heat disintegrating me. I saw orange and red flames leap into the air releasing the black rolling smoke of toxic death. I squeezed my eyes closed to let go of the thought. The air was thick with anticipation and sweat. If I was going to die on duty, this could be the day.

Flashes came in vivid bits and pieces as I tried to absorb the intense situation. My eyes searched the crowd of people, the leveled house, the plane, my truck, the paramedics, and the survivors. My mind kept assessing and reassessing as I held tightly onto the handline.

Spectators had gathered in awe and now numbered in the hundreds. If this plane exploded, we were all going up with it. I kept thinking, "Why don't the police push these people back?" My mind flashed back to my black boots on the floor of the fire station where I had kicked them off. I felt the emptiness of the stall.

I needed to change my position and climbed through the ice water-glazed, razor-sharp metal and wrecked construction covered with lightwater until I reached the center of what was once the roof of the leveled house. The pressure from the charged fire hose added to the difficulty of holding my position on unreliable terrain for long periods of time. In addition, the seal around the nozzle was leaking water and soaked my gloves. Even at the unseasonably warm temperatures of 40 degrees, my hands were freezing. A sharp motion caught my eye and I was surprised when an observant spectator threw me his gloves. I only glanced down momentarily to see his face, a middle-aged man who nodded at me. I barely acknowledged the kind person because I was so focused on the paramedics and the situation. His gloves were work gloves and not fire-retardant so I left them where they landed near me in the wreckage. I felt bad.

I moved again and positioned myself beside the rescue workers who were removing twisted metal and wreckage to free the pilot and copilot. Both were still alive. First, the paramedics and firemen removed the copilot. It took another hour to rescue the pilot, and yet another long hour to remove the loadmaster's body. He'd been trapped between the cargo and the bulkhead.

When I was relieved of duty four hours later, I was exhausted.

I later read the incident report by the Anchorage Fire Department. "There was no explanation as to why there was never a fire. By all rights and means there should have been. All of the elements were there: the power was on in the house, the natural gas line had ruptured, and the plane was loaded with 1,200 gallons of flammable aviation fuel. If the crash had caused just one spark, three homes would have been destroyed and all three crew members would have died. If the explosion had been delayed, it would have taken numerous rescue workers and spectators with it."

Several days after the crash, the widow of the loadmaster contacted our Chief and wanted to visit the wreckage where her husband had died. She wanted to say a prayer, mourn her loss, and extend her last good-bye.

I was working that day in a small rescue rig when the Chief had me pick up the widow at his office in the terminal building and drive her to the aircraft where it had been relocated to the south side of the airfield. When I arrived in his office I found a woman in her forties dressed in a pretty white blouse with soft lace, a black gabardine straight skirt and a black cotton cardigan. Even with the 2-inch heels on her boots, I still lowered my eyes from 5 foot 6 inches to look at her face.

I hesitated. This assignment was bringing up the emotions I had so successfully suppressed in working the crash. This was confronting grief in the face. It brought it too close to me.

I turned my back to the Chief and stared outside the large windows of his office that faced the west side of the apron area. The foggy weather prevented me from seeing Station Two on the west side of the airport. Suddenly I wanted to be there; at the one-man station, remote. Away from the frenzy of the main terminal building where hundreds of aircraft come and go and thousands of people are moving.

When I regained my focus, I wondered what I was supposed to say to her. That I was there when they pulled his body out? That I saw his lifeless face, his broken pieces? Of course, I would say none of this. Instead, I would shelve these memories—suppress them in the back of my mind.

We left the Chief's office and I drove her to the site. The weather was nasty—mixed rain and snow had covered our world in a gray, wet blanket and cutting any clear visibility.

When we arrived at the remains of the aircraft, I stayed in the truck as she stepped out to lay flowers on the wreckage and say a prayer. I watched her through the window of the small quick-response fire truck; my throat tightened as I thought of her grief. Memories of days prior filled my mind and I wondered where she had been at the moment of impact? Home, safe, unsuspecting; innocent. Then her phone rang and her life as she knew it had ended. I withdrew inside myself, shifting in my seat. I couldn't go there. I didn't want her to hurt.

No tears allowed.

When she sat back in the truck, she gazed at the dashboard without seeing. I could sense her rationalizing and trying to make sense of why he had died.

"If he hadn't ducked under the panel to protect himself, he might have survived."

I listened quietly, trying not to see the picture. But her words seeped into my consciousness. I swallowed hard and put the truck in gear.

We rode back in silence, her watery eyes searching outside the fogged up window—trying to find closure.

For me to be able to keep my sanity in these situations, I focused on doing my job as expected... and hoped the nightmares didn't follow. To alleviate the trauma from the horror and stress we were exposed to, we would bounce stories off our fellow firefighters and hoped our black humor would ease the memories.

But it never did.

The award and recognition of the firefighters who responded to the Chase YC-122 crash felt extraneous to me. As I received the Commendation for Bravery I thought of the small woman whose life was forever changed in an instant. No commendation would ever erase the pain I felt that day when I watched her place fresh cut flowers on the cold, twisted metal grave.

Chapter Thirteen

1968

My mother stood in our laundry room and I don't even know what precipitated my violent response. The trigger could have been either physical or verbal coming. Regardless, at age 16, I struck back for the first time. My mom was fifty-five years old. She was shorter than my 5'6," but not by much. And she was heavier than me. But she was strong because I had seen her fight. I had seen her take her casted arm, broken from a fall on the ice, and completely break a solid wooden bed post from its base.

I had never hit one of my parents. I was strong. I had learned how to fight. I wasn't afraid to fight. I was angry and fueled by so many years of verbal, emotional and physical abuse that I let go. Right there in the laundry room—just her and I. And when I hit her, I was surprised she didn't go down. Then I hit her again and again and again, pounding on her arms, her shoulders with both my fists gripped in a rage I couldn't control. I was screaming at her, maybe out of my own fear. I hit her so hard, she bounced against the wall but she didn't go down. I wanted to hit her face. I wanted to hit her stomach, make her hurt, but I couldn't. I stopped.

She never hit me back. She didn't even protect herself.

She knew.

1977

Captain Edwards' call came late one evening while I was relaxing and watching TV at our new house. Tim and I had moved from the small condo to a large house overlooking part of Cook Inlet. Too big, really, for two people and I didn't care for the house. It was a hodge-podge structure and sat alone on the outskirts of Anchorage. I wanted a neighborhood, surrounded by "Leave it to Beaver" people. I felt isolated on the outskirts of town. I wasn't old enough to want to be this alone.

"Hello." I said.

Captain Edwards started, "Hi, Maggie, How are you?"

I recognized his voice immediately. *Oh, no, I thought. Why are you calling me?* I didn't answer him.

"Have you read this evening's newspaper?"

No, I thought. *I don't even get the paper. Get to the point!* "No, I don't get the paper." I said calmly.

"You better go get one."

"Why?"

"You're on the front page. Just go get one then call me back."

A string of cuss words zoomed in my head and I was hoping none of them would come screeching out of my mouth while I was holding onto the receiver with my Captain.

What could I have possibly done now?

"Okay I'll call you back," I said.

I threw my coat on and walked outside. I swore out loud. Always something, always something! I have no peace in my life! I slammed the door to my black Ford sedan, an upgrade from my old Valiant, and raced off to the nearest store to get a paper.

I had worked the day shift on the lower level of the Terminal Building and we had been having trouble with the cabs. The newspaper clipping cited a cab driver's complaint that he never got a ticket receipt in exchange for the 50 cents it cost for him to pick up passengers at the airport. He was accusing Airport Police of taking that money.

But it was more than that.

Missing cash receipts at Anchorage International Airport resulted in a personnel shake-up, reported the *Alaska Advocate*.

$56,000 missing.

"Coin collected by security personnel was left in the coffee room uncounted and unattended during working hours," the audit report said. "...the safe (in security) was left unlocked... (and) all accounting personnel had keys to the accounting office and the combination to the safe."

It was a very sloppy and lax way to operate the accounting system.

My department was targeted and, as officers (the newspaper referring to us as security guards), one of our duties was to escort accounting personnel to each parking meter on the upper level of the airport. They opened and poured out the meter coins into a satchel we strung across our shoulders. After a while, with the weight of the coins, it was difficult for me to even walk in a straight line.

Then I would swagger to the Accounting Office where the coins were poured into a counting machine. I seldom stuck around, nor was I required to watch the accounting personnel count the money collected. Nor were we responsible for getting a receipt. In retrospect, that was bad business.

An internal investigation by the Alaska State Troopers was requested.

"Sit down." The investigation interviews began. The Alaska State Trooper gestured me toward a seat.

I stood in the small Chief's office in the fire station. I was in police uniform, on my way to my assigned duty. "I won't be staying long, so I won't be sitting." I dared to say, "What is it you want?"

"We need to read you your Rights. Miranda." The State Trooper's agitation was evident. I didn't falter under his intimidating stare. Then he read me my Rights.

"I refuse to talk to you," I said. "Start your investigation at the top (management), then work yourself down to us peons. Unless you do, you waste your time interviewing any of us."

I was the first to refuse the Trooper's questions. I was standing alone and the first. I knew my Rights—explained it a million times to suspects before I interviewed or arrested them.

I was released to go on duty.

I read the article and called Captain Edwards back. The cab drivers were agitated that they had to sit in line at a ticket—spitter (machine that spits out the tickets and stamps the times for parking), then one at a time come to the lower level to pick up passengers. If we didn't control that, we would find a multitude of cabs on the lower level at once, taking passengers out of turn. It was a first come/first serve process for the cabs and they liked to 'jump the spitter' (go around it). Regardless, allegations that our department was embezzling $56,000 dollars gave the cab drivers a reason to bitch about how we controlled their lineup. A ready excuse! The airport cops are not to be trusted!

Consequently, because of our bad press reviews, we had numerous incidents not only with the cabs but the public who accused our department of mishandling and stealing $56,000.

"Hi, it's Maggie." I returned the phone call to Capt. Edwards.

He asked, "Did you read the article? Was it you that the cab driver referred to?"

"No," I said. "I've never taken money and not given a ticket in return. The cabbies are using this $56,000 scandal as a reason to bitch about their situation. They don't like sitting in line."

"Okay," he said, "I believe you." And he hung up.

Although no public apology was given, the investigation regarding the embezzlement took almost a year and found no fault with our Department.

Chapter Fourteen

1963

My early years were not the worst of childhoods, but for me they were filled with confusion and fear. When my mother took a gun and put it to her head, yelling, "I don't want to live anymore!" it unnerved me. The three of us children grabbing for her hand, for the gun, for safety. *Please don't die, Mom.*

Why was she so unhappy? I wondered.

A mystery. I blamed myself for her unhappiness. Hoping to fix her, I tried to be perfect.

1978

I'd given up coming to work in uniform because I didn't like the different rules. I opened my locker and took off my coat. I slipped off my shoes and placed them on the bottom shelf, then started to take off my blouse. My eye caught a slight movement from under my winter uniform hat. But I dismissed it and continued to undress, and my hat moved again.

I yelled out, "Hey, guys! Why is my hat moving?"

I heard rustling behind me but no response.

"Hey, you guys! Did you put a mouse under my hat?"

Tim was getting off duty. I turned to him and stared with my hands on my hips. "Did you put a mouse under my hat?"

He grinned. "I don't know what you're talking about, Maggie." He turned away and faced his locker, smiling.

"I see that stupid-ass grin on your face, Foster."

Tim had recently been promoted to Sergeant and our supervisor/subordinate relationship was tricky. We tried to keep under the radar, low profile but that was impossible. Regardless, we continued to work together when the shift schedule dictated it and we continued to work emergencies. The nepotism waiver I submitted and was denied specifically stated we could not be promoted or supervise each other. Again, as long as we were not married, the State, in turn, ignored us.

I quickly replaced my blouse with the police uniform shirt and buttoned it. I stepped backward and swung my hand across the hat on the shelf, causing it to fall to the floor. The furry little critter scurried away.

"Okay you guys, which one of you sick puppies did this?"

No one spoke up, but they giggled like schoolgirls in the background.

I stepped out into the aisle and turned. "Is this how you guys bond? Can someone please help me pick up these turds?"

More laughter was the only response. Was I finally being recognized as part of the team? It was silly fun, but important in breaking a barrier. At least this time it wasn't a man crammed into my locker!

I carried my briefcase and utility jacket to the kitchen for roll call. Bob Leger came and sat beside me.

"Are you assigned to Engine Five, Bob?" I questioned.

"Yep. Hey, look at that new guy."

I followed Bob's stare to a young man in civilian clothes, with long blond hair to the shoulders. "He's got high heels on!" I exclaimed. The young fair fellow with Swedish looks was wearing three-inch platform shoes, and he was already six-feet tall.

Despite mumbling disapproval from the men, he silently slipped among us. I was impressed with his composure, went over and reached out my hand. "Hi, I'm Maggie. Welcome."

"Carlton."

"Carl?"

He reached for my hand and he corrected me. "No, Carlton."

"Okay, Carlton," I smiled. "Get a haircut."

"I know," he answered softly and smiled. "I didn't have time."

I liked Carlton right away. "Aren't you supposed to be in uniform?" He looked so out of place in civilian clothes.

Quietly, like he was embarrassed said, "Didn't have time for that, either. They called me at midnight to report for duty. I didn't even know I was hired."

"You mean you worked the graveyard shift already?"

He nodded. "Yeah. Actually, I'm leaving now."

Carlton went home and the rest of us filed out of roll call. Our team of four took a patrol car to the domestic terminal building where we were assigned. Two would work behind the airline gates overseeing the screening process. The other two of us patrolled on foot on the upper and lower levels of the Terminal Building. I thought about what my evening shift would bring. We could usually count on a call or two involving some kind of altercation.

Sure enough, before long we got a call to respond to the Upper One bar, located on the second floor. The call was to remove several unruly drunks. It's always tricky entering a bar, because you need time to adjust to the darkness. Jarrod stood beside me at the entrance.

"I'll go in." I said. "You'll know if I need backup." It wasn't that I was brave going in alone. Overkill could escalate the situation. With people who were drunk, I wanted to stay low-key because I found intoxicated people to be very unpredictable. My objective was to get them out quietly and without a major disturbance.

Jarrod agreed and I walked in and spoke to the bartender. I realized he was the man who had denied me a job three years before when I returned from touring the Lower 48 and was a certified bartender.

In 1973 I had walked into the Upper One bar at Anchorage International Airport to ask for an application:

"We don't hire women," he had replied and sneered at me like I was dirt.

"I have a bartending certification out of Denver. I've worked as a bartender in a speed bar and a restaurant in two different states."

The man looked directly at me as he stood behind the bar, his older eyes dull and unimpressed with my training or experience.

"Again," he stared, "we don't hire women."

Refused to even give me an application.

Now here I was a cop. I smiled. I was in police uniform, listening to him as he explained the situation in the bar. Nine hundred sixty hours of training. Carrying a gun. Qualified, trained, having the authority to take away a person's civil liberties. Here to rescue him. A woman.

But I couldn't be a bartender.

He pointed the other side of the bar. "Those guys over there. All five of them. I'm not serving them anymore."

I thought, *you can't handle drunks?* I couldn't believe I was talking to this jerk. He didn't recognize me, and I desperately wanted to tell him.

Sometimes I don't like being mature, but I let it go.

I walked to the table of men. "The management has asked you all to leave. And that's what you need to do now."

I watched for their response. They talked among themselves, and then wanted an explanation.

"You are loud and disorderly, and the management has asked you to leave, which they have the right to do. If you don't leave at this time, we will arrest you for trespassing. Pretty simple. So I would think about it before you decide to cause any trouble. It's not worth your while; believe me. You are not going to be served any more liquor. You can contact the day manager tomorrow morning if you feel like you've been picked on."

That was about as much diplomacy as I could handle. It almost worked. Four of them got up, grumbled and moaned, but they left.

One remained. He refused to leave. So I did the unconventional. I went up behind him and leaned over for him so he could smell my perfume. Then I whispered into his ear, "I'm going to leave now, but when I come back in here in five minutes, if I find you still here, I will arrest you for trespassing. Is that clear?"

I wanted to leave him his dignity. He didn't want a cop, even more so, a young female cop, age twenty-six; to tell him what to do.

When I came back three minutes later, he was gone. I was thankful for no fight, no arrests, and that I had resolved the situation. This girl.

The bartender nodded thanks. I dismissed him and walked out. Okay, not so mature this time. Then I remembered my interview question: How do you compensate for not being a man?

Chapter Fifteen

1978

The graveyard shift was always a challenge for me just to stay awake. Working those hours, midnight to 8 a.m., made my stomach queasy. I never felt rested, never knew if I was eating dinner, lunch or breakfast. And if I worked that shift during the summer hours, it was hard to sleep during the day with 19 hours of sunlight. But if I worked graveyard shift in the winter, I never saw the sun until my days off. It was too slow for me. But we were still rotating shifts and days off every 28 days.

I reported for duty at 11:15 p.m. I would be on patrol in a vehicle this shift that would help with my attitude since I did like that position the best. I liked being in a patrol car by myself so I could regulate my day as I wanted. And I liked being alone.

The winter night was cold at 13 degrees. I pulled the patrol car into stall one, which was kept empty. The car could thaw out while I got dressed.

Standing in the locker room by myself, I pulled on the snug men's white t-shirt then slipped on my men's navy blue uniform trousers over my long-johns. I didn't buckle my black belt or zip my pants because I had two more layers to tuck in.

I took out my bullet-proof vest and slipped it over my head. Custom made to fit perfectly. I checked the slash plate, which is located center chest to protect the heart from the penetration of a knife. All good.

I looked for my uniform shirt, tucked among four other shirts hanging in my locker. Three police shirts, one fire shirt. I grabbed the long-sleeve shirt and put it on. Our shirts were handsome. Medium blue, dark blue cuffs and dark blue flaps over each breast pocket. Dark blue lapels. We had silver removable buttons we had to take off every time we had the shirt dry-cleaned.

I buttoned the shirt up leaving the top button undone for my tie to be put on later. Military creases, looked sharp.

First I tucked my t-shirt into my pants, then the tails of my vest, then my uniform shirt. It took me a minute to get it all smooth and straight. Then I buckled my trousers, zipped up my pants and secured my belt. I could still see my waist. An important feminine factor for me. I never wanted to look mannish.

On the shelf in front of me was my collar brass. Actually silver. ASP: Airport Security Police. Originally, it was the old Alaska State Police insignia, as well as our badges.

I found my silver pen and pencil set that my mother had given to me for Christmas. And along with that, I grabbed my keepers, which were leather straps that snapped around my gun belt, holding it to my pant belt. Then my tie and tie clasp. Found them all on the top shelf. I grabbed my gun belt and went into the bathroom where the mirror was. I put the ASP insignias on, buttoned my shirt, put on my clip-tie, and swung my basket-weave gun belt around my waist.

I clasped the keepers and secured the gun belt tight. Then I drew my gun and checked the cylinder. It was loaded with .38 plus P's. Hollow point—designed to enter the body and mushroom. No exit. I replaced the gun into my front-break holster.

I went back to my locker, took out my utility jacket and checked the pockets. Gloves were inside. I found my officer's notebook, quickly flipped through it to see if I needed a new one. Catching my attention was a Swing Shift entry while I was on patrol a couple months prior. I had responded to an accident in which a construction worker fell two stories onto a concrete floor. The Anchorage Police Department didn't have anyone to respond so asked if we could since it was close to airport boundaries.

I was the first on scene and the man lay on his stomach with blood coming from his ears and mouth but he was still conscious. His eyes were open as I knelt beside him and quietly told him not to move, that the paramedics were on their way.

The second responders were the Anchorage Fire Department, then, finally the paramedics. I moved away as they took over.

I never did know whether the man lived or not but I kept thinking of his wife, who was about to join him with his dinner. I wanted to leave before she came.

I closed the notebook and tucked it in my right back pant pocket.

I reached down to the lower shelf to get my briefcase and laid it on the floor where I could quickly check to see if I needed any new forms: Rights form, accident, impound, investigation, etc.

As I closed the briefcase, I stood up and reached for my nightstick and put it in the ring on my gun belt. Then I grabbed my bunkers and walked out to the stall where the patrol car was parked.

The night was quiet and roll call was still 10 minutes away. I had time to check the fluids of the car so I wouldn't waste any time after roll call.

I checked the oils, fluids, radios, siren, and lights. I went to the Alarm Room and checked out the 12-gauge shotgun and a radio. I made a final trip to my locker to see if I had everything. Then I lock it. Oops, I forgot something. My parka. It was a man's parka, of course and way too big for me, but if I got stuck working traffic I'd need it.

Roll call. The shift began.

When I was patrolling in the middle of the night and was tired, I looked for anything that would hold my interest and keep my eyelids open. At three in the morning, on the south side of the airport, a car parked cockeyed in the street gained my full attention.

I drove up behind the car, called in my location, and pointed my spotlight directly onto the car's inside rearview mirror. I saw one person on the driver's side – not moving, not responding… to the flashing red lights or the spotlight.

My level of awareness boosted. With my flashlight in my left hand, I got out of the patrol car and unbuckled the security strap on my gun holster. I walked to the left on the driver's side, stopped just behind the driver's left shoulder, and leaned over slightly. I saw another person, a woman, with her head between his legs and his hands on her head. We'd had a rape in the Terminal Building less than a week prior and I was on edge. I banged on the window.

Dispatch was sending a second officer to my location.

The man brought the woman's head up. Her face was flushed and it looked as though she had been crying.

I stepped back, drew my gun and pointed it at the driver. "Get out of the car!" I commanded.

His slow reaction escalated my thought that this might be an assault. I repeated my demand. "Get out of the car!"

He put his shrinking privates back into his pants and stepped out of the car. I grabbed him and put him against the car. While I was searching him, I asked the woman, "Do you want to be here?"

She didn't answer, so I demanded in a louder voice, "Do you want to be here or not? Answer the question!"

She finally said, "Yes, I want to be here."

I immediately realized it wasn't an assault but a consensual sex act. I couldn't cancel my back-up request fast enough. If the guys got wind of this, I'd be toast.

But the back-up arrived before I finished my traffic stop. Then he made it back to the station before I did.

I took identification from both the man and woman, made sure he was sober enough to drive, and let them go.

Humiliation travels fast. "What's the matter, Maggie? Scare ya?" greeted me as I entered the kitchen at the fire station.

I tossed my hat onto the radiator. "Hey!" I muttered, "If you came across something that big, you'd have drawn your gun, too!"

More laughter. I was never going to live this down.

It was 4:30 a.m. and I stayed in the kitchen for about 20 minutes to eat before I got my next call. The dispatcher opened the intercom that echoed into the kitchen.

"Hey Maggie, do you know where the Coast Guard lighting area is off of Northern Lights?"

"Vaguely," I answered.

"APD (Anchorage Police Department) doesn't have anyone to respond and they have a fight in progress. You're it, kid."

I left the kitchen without asking anymore questions and wondered if I could find this secluded area, which overlooked Cook Inlet. I left with red lights on, no siren.

I edged my car onto the narrow pathway leading up to the crest overlooking the Inlet. The remote area, simply known as the Coast Guard lighting area, (an aid to maritime navigation), was a densely wooded area.

I slowly pulled my patrol car to a stop on the incline. I heard several people screaming at each other. My calls for a backup were unheeded. No one available. I was on my own. *You're it, kid!*

I stepped out of the car, took the shotgun out and told everyone to "Shut-up and come forward. Police!" The rotating red lights on my vehicle were the only lights besides the spotlight I had on them. Beyond the reach of the illumination lay the unknown, shielded by the cold blackness of night.

My voice of authority echoed through the heavily forested area as the words faded amongst the leaves. No one listened – until I jacked a round into the 12-gauge shotgun and yelled, "Everyone come forward!"

I repeated, "Party's over, folks; move forward!" As people began to gather within the artificial light of my spotlight, I counted six. Then I saw the damage.

The knife wound that sliced deep enough to show meat on one man's upper arm caught my attention immediately. After initial questioning I learned that his opponent was introduced to a two-by-four that was shoved up under his nose. Blood everywhere.

Time was a killer. I was dumping questions into empty space hoping for enough time to pass for someone to figure out I seriously needed help. Although I was relatively calm, it was almost impossible to keep the attention of people that had checked out of reality some time ago. They were still in a combative mood. I rolled out a battery of questions to keep them occupied.

Eventually, the station sergeant arrived and we managed to get everyone back to the fire station.

I interviewed them then call the Assistant District Attorney, the A.D.A., who, at that time, would make the final decision whether we should arrest or forward the paperwork to them to sort out. File a Complaint later. Too many unreliable witnesses.

The man with his nose on sideways went with the paramedics, but the man with the open knife wound refused treatment.

Let them go. Forward the paperwork. Sift through the mess.

Chapter Sixteen

1963

Junior High School brought on a whole new challenge. The first day of school, I wore pants, knowing that girls were supposed to wear dresses—a rule to be broken, scrutinized, demolished. The teacher told me not to come back the next day wearing pants.

My defiance had begun to develop.

I loved my blue wide-corduroys and proudly pranced around in them on the second day of school. I was nervous about my rebellion but stood firm in my belief that wearing skirts was the stupidest thing girls had to do here in Alaska.

I was released from school. "Don't come back," the principal told me, "until you understand the rules."

1979

My natural curls either had to be cut in a man's hairstyle, or grown out long enough to pin up off my uniform collar. My distain for this policy put me on the brink of insubordination.

Captain Grant was specific about how my hair should look – though I never received it in writing, and the never-ending warnings from various supervisors didn't keep me from continuously pushing to find the limit.

I'd pin up my hair for a while, then let it creep down below my collar, lower than allowed. Besides, pulling back my curly hair was almost impossible.

It's not that I never tried to conform. I did. I pulled all of my hair up and away from my face, above my collar into a "puff-ball" on top of my head. Shorter pieces of hair popped out all over as each strand of curl took pride in its individuality. I looked like a scarecrow, with wayward strands.

One evening, as I was approaching the patrol car for night shift duty, Lieutenant Corey called out, "Maggie, hold on."

I reluctantly turned.

"You can't wear your hair like that. Someone could grab your ponytail. You need to fix that before you go on patrol."

It was too short to be a ponytail. "Right," I said and turned away. *This is crazy!*

The following morning, I called a beauty parlor and made an appointment for a hairstyle. Following my insubordinate reaction to Lt. Corey's request that pulling my entire bush of curls into a puff ball wasn't enough to adhere to current hair standards, I received a written reprimand from Captain Grant. Along with the diagram of a man with a military haircut and mustache and sideburns, I was told, "Adhere to these standards."

Working the swing shift, I didn't report for duty until 4 p.m. My hair appointment was at noon so I had plenty of time to get the right hairstyle before my shift began.

I told the beautician, "This hairstyle needs to be above my collar, and I need to be able to get my hair underneath this hat." I handed her my Stetson. "I can't have sideburns below my earlobes."

She was innovative. "We could do ringlets, bring it up above your collar. Since your hair is naturally curly, we'll put ringlets in front of your ear. I'll make it above the earlobe, no problem."

I agreed. In the 1970s, ringlets were in again, forty years after Shirley Temple had ringlets. Mine would be tighter and not so bouncy.

When it was over, I tried on my hat. Cool. It looked good. Feminine. "Okay," I said with a smile. "Thank you so much. "This will work." I could adhere to the hair standards and still look like a woman.

I went to the fire station feeling good about my hair as I changed clothes. Management might even be impressed.

Before roll call, I walked into the bathroom. One of the sergeants was using the urinal. "Hi, Russ," I greeted. By now I recognized most of the men by their backsides. I always said something to them so they could zip up before they turned around.

"Whoa, that looks nice. Can you get your hat on?"

"Oh, yeah. I made sure of that."

I made a few adjustments and asked Russ, "What do you think?"

"Looks good. Looks great."

His comment made me feel secure.

At roll call, Lieutenant Corey standing behind the podium turned to me. "Maggie, put your hair behind your ears."

"What?" I asked with astonishment.

"Put your hair behind your ears. You don't have sideburns."

I was livid. Instinctively, I told him that I wouldn't.

His anger escalated. "Report to the captain before you go on duty!"

I left roll call furious and petrified at the same time. The confrontations were endless. I thought they would stop after I left home.

All I wanted was to perform my duties. But I was in a constant state of fighting for what I believed and being defiant of their treatment toward me. Much like my childhood years.

Captain Grant was in the alarm room. "I was told to report to you." I announced.

"Why?" he asked, obviously knowing the answer.

My indignation rose. "Something about Lieutenant Corey not being able to handle roll call."

"Pull your hair behind your ears, Maggie." He said matter-of-factly. Because he already knew what was coming.

I glared at him. "No!" This was a set-up, a conspiracy. There was nothing else to focus on but my sideburns or lack thereof?

His face reddened. He was barely holding it together. "Then get out of here!"

I did, though I knew it wasn't over. I got into the patrol car with four other officers, me in the back and we headed to the terminal building.

Mike Marshall offered a compliment, "You smell good, Maggie."

I didn't respond, although the simple remark made me feel good.

Inside the terminal, I took my post. Five minutes later, two officers came down. Ron said, "Chief wants to see you, Maggie."

I didn't move because my brain was trying to absorb the seriousness of a stupid situation. "So, it takes two of you to relieve me? I must be important, huh?"

Mike touched my shoulder, "Give 'em hell, Maggie."

They laughed, but with a mixture of sympathy.

Chief Hynes's office was just down the hall. I reluctantly walked slowly down the concrete corridor and mumbling I was about to face the warden. Alone with no one else to take a fall, I decided to push the limits all the way.

The Chief's secretary gave me a warm welcome and asked me to wait. I did, twenty minutes. This was part of the game: let me stew, get me nervous. No problem there. I was a nervous wreck.

Then the Chief entered. "You need to put your hair behind your ears, Maggie."

"You gave me a picture of a man's haircut, and my hair is not below my earlobes."

"You're not a man," he said.

"Then why give me a picture of a man and tell me to adhere to those regulations?" My nervousness was compounded by irritation. "You know, Chief, this is a stupid reason for me to be standing in front of you."

He raised his voice, "What is it you want, Maggie? Huh? What is it you want?"

I raised my voice, "Okay, Chief. You tell me how many warnings you give me before you reprimand me then how many reprimands do I get before you fire me!" *What did I just say!*

"You don't want to do that, Maggie."

I missed the justice in his statement.

I turned to him and calmly stated. "Yes, I do. That is what *I* want."

I couldn't believe my words. Although I was shaking, I found strength. My heart was pumping energy into my cause; I wasn't going to coward down. I was ready to fight. I wasn't going to quit. I'd let them fire me first.

Then, without warning, the Chief walked out. I couldn't come up with a reason to stay in his office, so I walked out, too. I went back to my post and I did not change my hair. There were no more confrontations about my hair that day.

The next day, I drove to the Human Rights office and filed a discrimination complaint against the State for the hair regulations: reverse discrimination. If the department had given me a picture of a man's military haircut, including sideburns and mustache, then why couldn't I have curls in front of my ears as long as they did not go below my earlobe (as in the picture). The woman said this was the first complaint of its kind she had seen. Usually, the men filed to have longer hair. I just wanted sideburns.

After taking my claim she told me to check back if I started getting covert harassment. I laughed out loud.

Then she told me this type of complaint had a two-year wait list.

Chapter Seventeen

1979

The winter fog around the entire airport was so thick that aircraft had difficulty finding their way from the runways to their gates.

The tower operator called me on the radio, "Ramp captain, Ground."

I was parked off Gate 26 listening to the radio transmissions between the various aircraft and the tower.

"Go ahead, Ground." I knew what he was going to ask.

"Yes, ma'am. It looks like we have a Pan American Airlines somewhere on the high-speed turn-off. I'm looking through the binoculars here, but I can't see for sure with the fog."

I visualized the man in the tower: about forty, white shirt, blue slacks, wearing a headset and holding a transmission button in his left hand, binoculars in his right. In front of him would be the board denoting the location of aircraft. He was twelve stories up, looking south. He was looking for one 747 and couldn't see it.

"Could you please see if you can locate him and bring him in to the east ramp?" he asked me.

It was a passenger flight, two-hundred plus people. It had stopped somewhere between the active runways, trying to find its way to the ramp but unable to see the markings clearly enough to proceed.

As the ramp captain, I was driving a small, quick-response fire vehicle with 500 pounds of dry chemical fire fighting agent. I carried fire gear and a gun. This was the only unit assigned to perform both fire and law enforcement duties.

I had no compass, only my knowledge of the runway layout and an understanding of the aircraft traffic. "Ground, I would like clearance across the east-west taxiway to the high-speed turn off."

"Roger, ramp captain. Hold short (don't cross the runway) for Flying Tigers 747.

I pulled the lever for my red lights and crept just short of the taxiway. I strained to hear the control tower radio traffic and turned down my station (police and fire) radio. This was incredibly dangerous, not having any visual references on foggy days, and tested my mental limits. Operating on sheer guts and instinct, hoping I wouldn't get lost. I had no ear protectors, so deciphering the radio traffic above the high-pitched whining of jet engines and propeller noise was an art.

"Ramp captain, you are cleared to cross the east-west taxiway and runway six-left.

"Roger, Ground. Thank you."

The thick milky fog wrapped around the airport. A jet blast from the fuel exhaust of the Flying Tigers 747 rocked my little vehicle. I proceeded cautiously, on full alert, trying to decipher the coming and goings of all the aircraft around me. Airplanes were taxiing, getting ready to take off. Some were landing; some were pushing back from the gates. A myriad of radio conversations squawked around me. I listened to the aircraft chatter, visualizing where each plane was.

I proceeded south. The tower operators couldn't see anything. They didn't have ground radar, which would have enabled them to track the aircraft. They depended on the pilots being where they said they were. If the pilots were lost, the tower depended on me.

"Anchorage Ground," I said to the tower, "I'm clear of the east-west taxiway and Six Left.

"Roger, ramp captain. Do you have sight of the aircraft?"

"Negative, Ground. I don't see him yet."

I was driving about five miles an hour. If I broke concentration I could immediately be lost. Adrenaline kept me focused.

Then I began to hear the familiar high-pitched whine of jet engines. I eased forward. I could tell they were at an idle. I could smell their jet fuel but I couldn't see the aircraft. *Where was it?*

Slowly, slowly...and suddenly I was facing the nose of the 747!

I jerked, almost hitting my head on the roof of my truck. The immense whining and suction of the 747's four engines conjured thoughts of being sucked up into the spinning vanes.

"Anchorage Ground..." I hoped he couldn't hear the shaking in my voice.

"Go ahead, ramp captain."

"Yes, sir. I've located the Pan Am on the high-speed. He is between six-right and six-left. Request permission to cross the runways and taxiways to the east ramp."

"Roger, ramp captain. Proceed with caution."

If I got too far ahead of the aircraft, the pilot could lose sight of me, so I drove slowly. My mind kept repeating: white lights are active runway lights; blue lights are taxiway lights. To make a mistake and find myself on the active runway would be disastrous. Even as I crossed the runways, I counted seconds to assure myself I was crossing them and not driving on them. The fog made me feel trapped and hidden. How did the air-traffic controllers operate under these obscure conditions?

The Pan Am and I cleared the taxiway and entered the east ramp. I located the ground maintenance who would guide the 747 into the gate. Finally relieved of my responsibility, I was spent. The foggy conditions that plagued our airport were always a menace.

In later years, a 747, while landing in foggy conditions, struck the back of a field-maintenance pick-up truck that was checking the braking action of the runway. One week after that incident, still in foggy conditions, a DC-10 collided with a Piper Navajo. The Anchorage Control Tower then finally received ground radar, three years earlier than scheduled. That enabled the operators to see all aircraft and movement on the ground under conditions where the naked eye could not. Not only did it make for a much safer airport, but it also alleviated a tremendous amount of responsibility and liability on the Airport Police and Fire Department. I found the assignment of guiding aircraft into the ramp on foggy days without GPS, compass or ear protectors incredibly dangerous.

Chapter Eighteen

1962

Into the glasses they poured ice cubes and whiskey. Captured in a tumbler of forgotten dreams. Captured in a tumbler of pain.

I could do nothing to stop it.

I was a born competitor and was searching for recognition as an individual. I didn't see much difference between boys and me.

My first attempt at competing with the masses was in a chess tournament in the fifth grade. The entire school of 600 was invited to play. My oldest brother taught me how to play and I was obsessed with it. Sometimes a game took me hours, which irritated my opponent.

"Hurry up, Maggie!"

But I was always studying the situation. I had plan A, B, and C already formulated in my mind. I was thinking three and four moves ahead, to trick my opponent into moving a certain way.

Chess is about knowing your opponent and speculating the moves. I was a master of that by age ten. After all, I lived in an alcoholic family. Anticipation was the name of the game.

I came in second. Beaten by a boy.

1979

I remember clearly the day I took mom to the doctor at Providence Hospital. I went into the room with her when she received her diagnosis.

The young doctor, who was substituting for mom's regular doctor while on vacation, faced us with his long, white coat. He was merciless in his statement that, "Yes, in fact, you have cancer."

We were both speechless. Then mom asked, "Is it malignant?" The doctor said matter-of-factly, "Yes, yes, it is."

I left mom with the doctor and walked across the skylight of the hospital, stopping in the middle. It was a beautiful day, spring—sunny and crisp. I was 28 years old, just four years after dad died.

I stood watching people below me thinking *everything just keeps moving*. But for my world it had stopped. The tears ran down my face as I tried to imagine what my mom was thinking. The cancer was in her mouth, probably caused by smoking.

I never developed a relationship with mom until she was diagnosed with cancer. I became the caretaker and I didn't mind. It was an opportunity to get to know her.

After an aggressive treatment of radiation, the cancer was under some control.

Celebrating the completion of her treatment, mom and I flew to Seattle to see her sisters and extended family. One day while visiting with mom's friends at a party, I made the comment to a woman who expressed a great deal of admiration for mom.

"She (mom) drinks too much," I said. It was a petty thing to say especially after the woman had complimented mom. I regretted it as soon as I said it.

The woman laughed and said, "Oh my dear, we *all* drink too much!"

I stood back and observed the party. Drinking, smoking, laughing. The people were dressed smartly and conversation was lively and intelligent. The house we were in was elegant with a large crystal chandelier over a high-sheen cherry-wood dining table. Seating for eight. The china cabinet set next to the table with a display of old and delicate plates peeking through the worn glass. I imagined the drawers were full of real silverware as well as antique silk napkins—maybe the 1920s era. The high ceiling was trimmed in crown molding; a classy display of art. I had not been exposed to much of anything this glorious in architecture. I immediately fell in love with the romantic richness of dusty scent from the past and the visual compliment of the present.

While absorbed in my surroundings, it occurred to me, as my eyes drifted between the people and cigarette smoke, the house and the activity, that this was the world my mother had come from. I had seen her many times sitting in the dark at home, late at night by herself, drinking, playing Frank Sinatra and Perry Como. She would sit for hours listening to the same songs. I never understood her behavior. I can only guess she stepped back in time and those songs brought her some happiness; memories of another time. Like this gathering.

She lived the safety and warmth and family, but then chose the darkness, remoteness and the cold of Alaska. Alaska was young and rough and unsophisticated. *Was it worth it to her?*

I turned my attention toward mom and watched her interact with relatives and friends. These people loved her. And my mom was often the center of attention with Alaskan stories and an easy laugh.

I had not seen this side of her.

In June of that year, the Department had firearms qualifications again. By then, I qualified twice a year and no longer practiced in between.

The timed competition was among seventy-five men, some who practiced religiously, and me.

We shot rounds at a stationary silhouette target, alternating between our strong and weak hand from various positions (prone, standing, kneeling). We began at the fifty-yard line, and ended at the seven-yard line. We could run the course twice, and choose the higher of the two scores.

For the qualification, I went to the firing range early on my day off, so I could take my time, less pressure. I usually took mom for a ride on my days off. The radiation treatments for cancer seemed to be slowing the effects of the disease, and I thought it important to keep her active. Today, I took her to the range. I wanted to show her something I was good at.

The summer day brought warm weather, high clouds, and no wind. Perfect conditions.

Regardless, the range officer, Captain Grant, always made me nervous. It was as though I still had to prove myself to him and weapons qualification seemed to be my ticket to earn his respect. If he respected me, the Department would respect me.

My mom sat in my car and watched. Only two other officers were at the range when I arrived. Three of us were allowed to shoot at the same time, so I didn't have to wait.

I loaded my gun behind the fifty-yard line, holstered it, and waited anxiously for the starting whistle. When it blew, I took a deep breath, ran up to the line, drew my weapon, and lay on my stomach. I shot six rounds with my right hand, reloaded, stood and shot another six rounds with my left hand.

I reloaded, put my gun in my holster and ran to the twenty-five yard line. As I blasted rounds at the standing target, suddenly I realized I was alone. Usually everyone advances to each stage at about the same time. As I was thinking that, Captain Grant tapped me on the back. "You didn't finish shooting at the fifty-yard line, Maggie. You have six more rounds standing up with your right hand."

Stunned, and my concentration blown away, I ran back to the fifty-yard line.

"Hurry!" he yelled. "You're on the clock."

I quickly shot the six more rounds, reloaded, holstered my gun – then ran back to the twenty-five. By now, I was so confused that I forgot to shoot my additional six rounds here, too.

"You've got six more rounds, Maggie!" Captain Grant yelled. "Left-handed."

Six more rounds left-handed, kneeling. Boom! Boom! Boom! Boom! Boom! Click.

Click? The gun didn't fire. The whistle sounded, and everyone holstered their weapons.

"Time's up!" hollered Captain Grant. "Advance to the fifteen."

"What?" I asked. "Didn't you hear that click? My round didn't go off."

Thank goodness he had heard it and he gave me another round. I shot one more. Boom!

I reloaded and walked up the fifteen-yard line. From there I could easily see where my bullets were hitting. Mostly in the center rings. I thought it looked pretty good, considering I'd been dancing to a tune no one else could hear. Seeing tightly grouped shots in the center encouraged me to refocus and concentrate on the remaining series of shots, which I did without any further episodes of disaster.

Grant walked to my target to calculate my score. He counted the bullet holes with his black permanent marker. "Not too bad," he said.

"Ninety-seven percent." I exclaimed.

"Well, we'll see," he said. "We still have another week. But who knows, maybe you'll be Number One."

His crooked smile eased itself across his heavy five o'clock shadow.

After the last week of weapons qualification, Captain Grant advised me that I had, in fact, placed number one in the Department. It was even on the bulletin board notice, along with the statement that I was the first woman to ever do so. It made me light-headed, giddy, as the men congratulated me. Almost accepted. No one seemed put out or disturbed. Tim and I always competed with each other. Since I had out-shot him, dinner was on him.

He stood in our kitchen. "We're going to Grant's house tonight for dinner."

"What? Are you serious?" I couldn't believe it.

Captain Grant had taken Tim under his wing, kind of a mentor training. They had developed a friendship and trust. Being involved with Tim brought me into the picture on a personal level with the captain.

In the five years I had been at the airport, Captain Grant had not said hello to me even once whenever he entered the locker room – although he made an effort to say hello to everyone else. Dinner on a personal level with someone who has deliberately oppressed my existence put me in a guarded position. Was he looking for more material to attack me? It was scary to be friendly with Captain Grant, but my curiosity was piqued. Maybe there was a real human being under all his meanness?

Although I was uncomfortable, I found him and his wife cordial and friendly.

After dinner, we sat on the couch and he handed me a present.

"What's this?"

"Open it."

I couldn't imagine what it could be. Maybe an apology for his consistent disrespect toward me?

I unwrapped the tissue paper and there in my hand was a trophy with a pistol mounted and engraved: "Margaret Holeman, Top Gun, Airport Police, 1979."

I could feel the water pooling in my eyes as my fingers delicately touched the imagery of achievement and acceptance.

Chapter Nineteen

1968

It wasn't just the physical confrontations. Worse yet was the emotional degradation that would last a lifetime. The silent abuse. To have your parents tell you they hated you and eat away at any self-esteem you ever thought could be possible. To be held or hugged became an exception to the rule, if ever. I've been called a whore and a queer by my own parents, and they believed both. And the accusations: being blamed for something you never thought of then having to suffer those consequences. I can't count the times I've been called stupid. I was always wrong, no matter what and your confidence floats away, slowly, but obviously. And forever. Into a deep whirlpool of emptiness.

1979

"Are you going to attend the fire school Maggie?" asked Carlton.

Standing at my locker, I finished pulling out my fire gear. "I think so. How about you?"

"Yes. Lieutenant Nebgen said I could stay on day shift and take Engine Five."

"So, when are you getting married, Carlton?" I had played matchmaker between him and a nice young lady several months ago and they seemed to be connecting quite well.

With his fair skin, the flush on his face was quickly visible. "I don't know. I haven't asked her yet."

"Well, when you do, don't forget who introduced you."

My relationship with Carlton had grown the last two years. He was a good friend. I was surprised at his ability not to cuss in a job filled with profanity. He was a gentle man who maintained his individuality even though the men teased him. I liked Carlton's ability to resist and I had a tremendous amount of respect for him.

Employed at the airport for five years now, I was very excited about attending the first aircraft crash-training in Anchorage. It would involve the actual burning of an airplane. Representatives from a variety of departments including the Anchorage Fire Department, Air National Guard, and Fort Richardson Army Base crash crews, and employees of local hospitals were attending. It was being held at our Fire Station One. The truck stalls had been transformed into a classroom. We would train forty hours over five days: class work for two days, a mixture of classes and fire training the third, a simulated crash on the fourth, then review and graduation on the fifth.

The fire chiefs from Denver's Stapleton International Airport and the Los Angeles International Airport would supervise. Local media covered the event.

I was assigned to Engine Three for the entire five days, a primary response truck for any actual incidents as well as for the simulated crash. I was the only woman and most senior in experience who would attend the training. I was honored to be on the front line. On the fourth day of the training, the old Constellation aircraft filled with 4,000 gallons of jet fuel would be ignited, initiating the mock crash and rescue.

On the fourth day, Chief Hynes stood in front and gave accolades for everyone's joint effort to coordinate the training. He then assigned us to the trucks for the simulated disaster. I was *reassigned* to Engine One, an old 1959 American LaFrance fire engine designed to only carry water, and the only truck to remain behind, "in case of an actual emergency."

I tried to comprehend the rationale for management taking me off Engine Three – replaced by a rookie employed only five months, still on probation, not even attending the training. A man.

My mind registered the assignment like a vacuum sucking me into the filth; I felt dirty, unworthy – particles of something discarded, unwanted—to get rid of. I averted my eyes. Glances from the firefighters told me that they also thought I was still assigned to Engine Three.

The blood drained from my face.

Carlton squeezed my shoulder. "Are you going to be okay?"

"Of course. Absolutely. Have fun, Carlton." I quickly turned away.

With an electrifying sense of anticipation, seventy people showed up at Fire Station One—the mock victims, crash crews, hospital personnel, and support units. Summer was in full swing and the mass gathering caused the dust to stir.

The excitement gathered momentum and the mass of people exited to the south side of the field where the mock disaster would take place. The trucks roared as each driver pressed forward.

From the fire stall, I watched them all leave. My anger and frustration rocketed. This was my school. This was my fire station, my truck assignment. I was asked to be in the first Mock Crash/Rescue Training. And as I stood there in the silence, in the dust, and the incomprehensible reason for being left behind, I knew I was going to cry.

I started pacing throughout the fire station. I walked outside so the dispatcher wouldn't see me.

He called for me on the intercom. "Maggie, you out there? What are you doing? Come up and see me."

I didn't respond.

"Maggie! Come on, come up here and talk to me."

He knew I was hurting. As I stepped into the kitchen, I could hear him still calling for me.

"Go away, just leave me alone!" I yelled into the intercom.

"Come on, Maggie, talk to me."

Despite Jack's sensitivity, I felt hostile. "Okay, Jack, I'll be back here doing dishes like a good little *girl* should be doing! So just leave me alone!" I started crying. I wanted to control myself, but I couldn't.

The sound of crutches on the tile came up behind me. The Dispatcher had called him; probably said I was a mess. Couldn't even respond to a real emergency.

"Maggie," Captain Grant said, "Lieutenant Nebgen and I will take your truck. You go on out there."

The sympathy in his voice was foreign to me.

He called Chief Hynes on his radio. "You want Officer Holeman out there?"

Through the muffled background noise and fury of activity, the Chief answered, "Right. Bring her out. Right."

"Go out there, Maggie." said Captain Grant, "That's an order."

"I'm not going!" I declared belligerently. "They switched trucks on me for a reason and you know it."

He quietly slipped out of the kitchen without continuing to push me.

John Tibor, who was working patrol, came into the kitchen shortly after Captain Grant left.

"Go away, John! I'm not going!"

John came and took my arm. "Maggie, I know they did you wrong, but, please, let's just go out there. The lieutenant is taking your truck."

I was ill-disposed, resentful even of the smallest acts of kindness. "Let me get this straight, John. A rookie took my truck, and a lieutenant is relieving me? And *now* it's okay for me to go out there? It's safe now, is that it?"

John Tibor had been sent in to gently guide me. The misguided, make her understand the rules. *We took your power.*

I went with him, not *out* of defeat, but to *feel* the defeat so I could remember it. So it could fuel my anger.

The fire had already been extinguished and they were in the process of transporting the mock victims to the local hospitals. The part I would have been involved in – extinguishing the bulk of the fire with Engine Three – was over. Irretrievable.

I didn't get out of the patrol car and John didn't pressure me. Watching the end of the simulated disaster made me feel disjointed, lost, still a child trying to understand why I was unaccepted.

As I entered my house, I thought about quitting. I wanted to. I called two friends for feedback.

"No," they both said. "Go back to work. Don't give up."

What does that mean? Why not just give up?

They stripped me of my confidence but more than that; it generated a sense of mistrust even after years of proving myself. Everything I had worked for was gone. Take her off the truck. Hide her. It wasn't just the five years I had crawled up to acquire some sense of self-esteem. It was the whole twenty-eight years of my life. Back on the chopping block. And I wasn't strong enough. I was back to square one.

I went back. After a sleepless night, I entered the classroom for the final day, my eyes swollen from crying, hiding behind sunglasses.

I noticed that my classmates were looking my way. Suddenly, they began to clap and applaud. They knew. Dazed, I worked my way back to my chair and sat next to Carlton. I waved slightly to thank them for their support, and then slipped back into my world of conflict.

Chapter Twenty

1957

I had to be six because he still lived at home and I could still remember. I sat on the edge of the porcelain bathtub in our downstairs bathroom, waiting for my brother Tiger to pee.

When he came into the bathroom, all I remember was him looking at me, then Tiger peeing then his powerful hands slammed me against the bathtub. My head hit the other side of the porcelain tub then I sunk down into the empty tub screaming.

He picked me up. I was holding onto my head where the swelling was obvious. My little legs were moving up and down his middle, still screaming.

Then he said, "Shhh, shhhhh. Don't tell mom."

1980

The late intense June sun penetrated the large Dispatch windows, the heat soaking into the room where I worked. On a quieter day, I would have opened the door to let a breeze circulate in the small building. But I had dispatched fire equipment to an airplane crash and closed the doors to muffle the sound of equipment leaving the station.

After the fire had been extinguished and all the units had returned, Ben Carey who was on the initial response, opened the door and walked into Dispatch. His portly body held a Polaroid picture for me to see. His face was placid, emotionless. He threw the picture in front of me.

I turned away from Ben, knowing he dared me to look at the photo. He didn't say anything. I knew this was some kind of gruesome test. Could I stomach the photo? When the picture landed on the console in front of me, I took a minute before looking at the man who had just died.

Instead, I looked outside the windows, losing myself in the activity of planes, vehicles, and people. I had sent Ben to a small aircraft, a PA-18, that had crashed just after take-off near Lake Hood. The plane had been totally destroyed in fire, leaving only the skeleton of the aircraft. Foamy light-water had smothered the fire and covered the plane.

I lowered my eyes to the photo, trying to be passive like it didn't matter. Before me the melting figure of a man burned in position with his hands still on the steering column, covered in white foam with skin dripping from his skeleton—his life dissolved.

Again, I looked away, searching for something normal outside the windows. Birds, people not dead, laughter.

At midnight, after I got off work, I drove to the crash site. The outline of the plane was black against the dim hue of purple and pink that hovered gently along the horizon giving people in their own worlds a last glimpse of the sky. They will ease their nights into soft sleep. But not me.

For my sky I saw the tail of an airplane tipped high as the aircraft nosed into the ground. Light-water and the burnt smell of aviation fuel pooled beneath the plane reminding me of the delicate time between life and death. It was always that burnt after-smell saturating and invading the air that I remember. And as I stood outside my car, I could smell the loss of life.

The man died on impact. And we could only pick up the pieces.

Chapter Twenty-One

1981

By 1981, Tim and I had lived together for five years. During this time, he had been promoted to Lieutenant, two levels higher than me. We had worked several emergencies together. As long as we didn't get married, the Department looked the other way, despite our supervisor/subordinate relationship. However, by taking no action, they gave me my defense for a nepotism waiver. I contacted a union lawyer and filed yet another complaint: discrimination against marriage. The union wanted to make our case a precedent.

Anytime I "stepped up to the plate" I could count on months of residual effects. Again, I entered that chaotic world. Working conditions were difficult. "Don't trust her; she's sleeping with a supervisor." Alienation.

Trying to keep equity in our professional relationship, Tim overreacted in his supervisory role. No favoritism. It seemed I washed more trucks than anybody! He was cautious not to cause waves. Don't give anyone a *reason* to complain. *Walk on egg shells.*

I wanted to get married. I didn't want to fly below the radar anymore. I was twenty-nine years old.

After months of meetings, interviews, questions and litigation, an unconditional nepotism waiver was issued to Tim and me. *Congratulations*, it said. You won. No conditions on your upcoming marriage. We could work together. We could be promoted. We could work emergencies together. A first for the Department. Changed the rule.

In April that year, Tim and I married at the Rabbit Creek Inn, which was often rented for special occasions. Big windows faced the water on the warm, spring afternoon, overlooking Potter Marsh. Fifty people showed up. Captain Grant was in charge of the music. Things were changing.

Mom stood over my shoulder as I sat at the wooden table to sign my new name on the marriage document. It had been a long haul for her. Dad had died. She was fighting cancer. She was sixty-nine.

Her hair was silver; her brown eyes dim behind large blue rimmed glasses, her red lipstick on perfectly. She wore a mauve-colored sweater with a matching pleaded skirt and a white blouse tied at the neck. She had lost so much weight that her skirt drooped to the floor, exposing her petticoat. She pulled it up and we laughed. I told her she looked gorgeous.

As she leaned over behind me while I was trying to decide how to write my new name, her Shalimar perfume crept into my space. How familiar that scent was. "Are you going to sign your name in the traditional form?"

"What exactly does that mean, mom?"

She answered with some pride, "You drop your middle name, take your last name as your middle name and take his last name as yours."

"I can do that, Mom. That sounds good, proper."

Although there was nothing traditional about my life, I still wanted to please her. So I changed my name and I think I made her proud that day.

Chapter Twenty-Two

1981

"What's the matter? Afraid to show a little ass?"

Said to me by a sergeant when I moved out of the men's locker room.

"Do you think you're better than us?"

Said to me by a fellow officer when I moved out of the men's locker room.

Throughout the years of using the same locker room as the men, I began to feel this bastion of males was accepting me and the locker room was a haven for bonding with them. During shift changes, chatter filled the room, kidding and jokes, stories of the day. They dressed and undressed, talked about guns, fishing, cars, and how they were in charge. They laughed, bragged, exaggerated. I grinned at some of their stories, scratched my head in confusion at others. Would I ever understand men?

Major budget cuts had occurred, causing massive overtime. Bonnie was hired six years after my hire date, 1980.

Bonnie was an independent woman, married to a state trooper and already familiar with law enforcement and bureaucracy. At five-foot-four, she was a firecracker when it came to her rights. I liked her.

She had been employed a year when she approached me about our locker-room situation. She and I were the only women in the department at the time using the men's locker room and bathroom.

"You know I'm going to a lawyer about the overtime, right?"

Mandatory overtime was an issue for Bonnie who had two small children and on-demand daycare didn't exist. Both she and her husband worked shift work.

I nodded, "So?" We were standing together in the kitchen.

"Well, do you think we should go ahead and also file a complaint to get out of the locker room?" She leaned over to me in anticipation of my agreement.

"You mean fight it."

Of course, fight it. Everything we get, we fight for.

"Yeah," she said. She nodded up and down to encourage me. "What do you think? Do you think it's about time?"

Bonnie was coming off the day shift and I was coming on the swing shift.

Instead of answering her right away, I said, "Let me get back to you, I need to change for my shift."

Then I walked away to my locker – where the rest of the men on my shift were changing.

I was assigned police duties in the terminal building and I was anxious for my shift to start. This was my favorite shift, the 4 p.m. to midnight. If anything exciting was going to happen, it usually was during these hours. The only assignment better than working in the terminal building was when I worked alone in a patrol car; call sign 603.

Tim Cronin, a tall, quiet spoken man about five years younger than I was my partner in the terminal building. I was assigned to the upper level and he to the lower level. It's important who your partner is in case all hell breaks loose, you can rely on your back-up. Tim was conscientious and a good officer. I trusted him, although I still considered him a rookie. He was four years my junior in seniority.

During the course of my duty that evening, I thought about what Bonnie proposed and I questioned why I even hesitated. Did I think I was going to sever the camaraderie? Why did I think the locker room even promoted any kind of bonding? All it provided was an opportunity to be exposed. Not to mention my constant vigilance of trying to dress inconspicuously. Then there was the touching where some men felt free to catch a pinch on my ass or rub up against me when they passed behind me to their lockers. And I knew Bonnie was right. For seven years I had been tip-toeing around the rules and discrimination.

As I stood staring at the large terminal building windows that cut the darkness of the outside, my thoughts were interrupted by Officer Tim Cronin, whom I could see his reflection as he approached me.

Tim started, "Hey, I saw you nodding. What are you nodding at? Who are you talking to, Maggie?" He laughed.

"Right, nobody. I talk to myself a lot, Cronin, that way I get no arguments."

"Okay, I'll be downstairs if you need anything."

"Got it," I said and watched him walk away, take the escalator and disappear.

I *was* nodding when Tim came up behind me. I nodded with a renewed commitment to once again take a stand. I'd tell Bonnie in the morning.

I walked down to the end of B Concourse, our newest concourse. My mind slipped back to the original structure of the airport. In the 1950s our C Concourse had actually been the entire airport. We used to walk out onto the tarmac to wave goodbye to our loved ones as they taxied off. Then we would turn our backs to protect ourselves from the prop wash of the DC-3s and DC-6s.

I walked to the large circle at the end of B Concourse where five airlines departed from the gates. Hundreds of people were leaving and coming into the airport late into the evening. It was 1981 and the Alaska Pipeline was still providing the energy of jobs as well as the crime and booze that comes with money.

I only had an hour before my shift was over when I received the dispatch:

"Attention 601, 602, 603 and 408 (patrol sergeant). We have a fight in progress at the bar, gun involved. All units respond."

The bar was located just around the corner from the beginning of the B Concourse. I was at the end of it, a good minute run. I didn't run at full speed knowing I had a ways to go. I ran trying to conserve my energy for a probable physical confrontation.

Then my mind raced as my legs pounded the commercial carpet. *"What if?"* scenarios whipped through my thoughts like the north wind coming off a glacier. Shifting scenes, changing answers, questioning my own competence.

Then I arrived. The two men who were fighting were wrapped around each other on the floor by the Alaska Airline's ticket counter back door. I knew most of the women that worked for Alaska Airlines and as I rounded the corner, I could see they were gathered to watch the events along with several people from the bar.

Then I heard one of the Alaska Airline employee yell, "Be careful, Maggie!"

I was first on scene.

A quick and immediate cursory search did not reveal a weapon.

I dropped to my knees onto the commercial carpet over concrete and wrapped my arm around the neck of the man on top. In my own heavy breathing mixed with the offender's sour sweat, I leaned over and yelled in his face, "Police! Let go of him!" It didn't work. They were both large men, tall and fit and tightly intertwined in each other with their own agenda.

With my arm still securely around the neck of the man on top, I yelled, "Where's the gun?"

And before anyone could or would answer, the surprise attack came from behind me when a woman physically jumped on top of me, sandwiching me with her on top and the three of us underneath. A pile of four struggling grown-ups.

Although it took the wind out of me, I managed to regain my senses quickly and shifted my body for enough leverage to swing backwards, my left arm making contact with a soft frame as I yelled, "Get off me!"

She hit the ground screaming, "There's no gun! That's my husband!"

As I turned my attention from the woman back to the sprawling men, I placed my right upper arm underneath the face of the man on top and supported it with my left hand for additional strength. Then I yanked his head sideways. And under complete control I said, "Release him. You are under arrest."

He let go.

Tim came up behind me, "I got him, Maggie. I got him."

I got up off the floor and we placed them both against the wall to search and hand-cuff them and arrested them for disorderly conduct.

Other officers arrived to help and the story unfolded. These were both military men: one an officer, one enlisted man. The argument was over a woman. It was the officer's wife that jumped me from behind and I considered arresting her for interfering. As it was, both men went to jail for disorderly conduct. Bad news in the military world.

After work several of us, fired up from the adrenaline events—the perfect ending and whew! We didn't get hurt—went to the bar down the street where we often met.

Tim was as wound up as I was and said, "When I heard the dispatch, I knew it would take me awhile to get there but I knew you could handle it. I knew you could handle it. I was taking the escalator three giant steps at a time!"

And with his long legs, I knew he was telling me the truth.

The beer flows, the stories ebb and laughter eases my anxiety. I thought how much I loved this job. The lights were low, the music loud and the laughter apart of a connection. I was sitting among seven other fellow officers drinking beer in local bar. We gathered after a shift—whether it was dynamic or stagnant—it didn't matter. What mattered was the connection afterwards. Camaraderie. An explosion of emotions, thoughts, opinions and bashing. It was about the completion of a shift, a feeling of welfare, of safety and accomplishment.

The beer. The booze. The boys. It helps for a period of time. It numbs my pain. It allows me to forget, and helps me laugh. It makes me flirtatious and gives me attention. It makes me feel accepted.

I love this life. I think I'm in heaven. And for those moments that the booze flows and I dance—the images of damaged goods disappear.

Then I wake up and the booze wares off, the stories fade and still—I'm empty.

Two days later Bonnie approached me in the locker room.

Do you still have that picture of the hair cut?"

Thinking of the picture of a man's military haircut that was given to me to conform to hair standards, I readily answered. "Oh, yeah. I do."

"Well, if you give that to me, we can take that to the lawyer and see if we can change the hair regulations as well."

"That would be nice," I said. I retrieved the picture from my locker and gave it to her.

Bonnie filed the complaint through a private lawyer. Two days later, I received a call at home from the airport manager.

The airport manager explains to me that Bonnie and her attorney took the complaint to the deputy commissioner, who brought it to him.

"I would like to hear your side of the story," the airport manager starts, "I didn't know you had to use the men's locker room. I didn't know until I was down there the other day. We'll take care of that. What about the bathroom situation? You never mentioned anything to me about that."

Funny, I thought, he was in the kitchen of Fire Station One less than a week ago while I was dressing for duty. He'd had a full view of me.

"Maggie, are you there?"

"Yes, I'm here," I finally answer. I start cautiously. "The Department of Labor is aware of our situation. As are Captain Grant, Chief Hynes and the entire department."

Memories of past harassments fueled my reaction and I threw caution to the wind and told him what I really thought. "Do you know what it's like to walk into a bathroom while a guy is using the urinal? Or I'm trying to take a shower and I'm not alone in the bathroom? Or I'm on my period."

He sighed. "I didn't know that was going on."

BS! I thought. You were just in the fire station watching me undress.

I wasn't finished. "Being equal doesn't mean acting like a man. I'm a woman, and there should be provisions for the differences.

He was quiet. "Okay," he says, "give me a couple of days. I didn't know things were that bad."

The next day, the airport manager and the assistant airport manager approach me in the terminal building while I'm working foot patrol.

"You have a minute, Maggie? We'd like to talk with you. Please sit down."

"That's okay, I prefer to stand. I'm on duty." They sat and I stood.

"Bonnie and I are not trying to create problems," I said. We're here to do a job, and we expect the same considerations as any employee. I have tried several times to correct the problems about the bathroom, the hair regulations, the locker room—but management is never willing to listen. It's too bad that push has come to shove, but we've been forced into it…and I don't feel bad at all."

They explained that they were considering giving Bonnie and me the Chief's office as a locker room and bathroom. I just stared at them. *Was it that simple? I had fought and put up with this for years. Now, boom, just because we have a lawyer?*

I call Bonnie and she screams into the phone. We didn't expect anything to happen this fast.

The next morning, Bonnie was working day shift and Captain Grant told her she and I were authorized to move our lockers into the Chief's office. That was a heavy and cumbersome ordeal. So, I came in early on the swing shift, and she and I did it together.

However, the Chief's office proved to be a very inconvenient location for everyone, so before long management authorized a storage area to be renovated in the first truck stall. It was spacious for dressing. Bonnie and I had a vanity area for make-up, our own bathroom with a shower, and six large lockers. I was in heaven!

Then the harassment began.

Over the next couple of weeks, when both Bonnie and I were working, the tell-tale signs of someone entering our locker room came in bits and pieces but always obvious. On different days we found the floor flooded with water, urination over the toilet, the toilet seat lifted, and a derogatory remark written on a picture of my husband inside my locker. I didn't feel it necessary to lock my locker given I was in a secure locker room. So, not only did someone enter a supposedly secure locker room, but entered my locker as well. After seven years on the department, I was astounded at the insensitivity and childish behavior. After seven years with the guys, I was shocked.

One morning, Bonnie handed me a brown bag containing a douche bag, Tampax, Kotex, FDS spray, and a colostomy bag.

"Where'd you find it?" I asked flatly.

Pointing into our locker room, she stated. "In the corner, over there, on the floor."

I grabbed the bag and told Bonnie I would be right back. Our area was supposed to remain locked. Bonnie and I had compiled a list of who was working and when...and only the on-duty supervisor had the other key.

I called the Chief and the airport manager and asked for a meeting immediately. Surprisingly, they complied.

Infused with resentment that the department allowed such blatant and unforgiving harassment and discrimination, I could barely talk. Instead, I slid the names of violators across the round table to my chief. Then I individually picked out the contents of the brown paper bag found in our locker room, I stated, "Here, Chief, have some Tampax. Mr. Chambers, here is some feminine hygiene spray for you."

My frustration and years of fighting for equality landed in front of my superiors. The remainder of the contents spilled onto the table as I stood. "Here are my conditions, gentlemen. I want one key and only one key to our dressing room. If I find anybody unauthorized has been in that room, I will sue the State for money."

The Chief explained that our locker room was, in fact, secure and a supervisor controlled that entry.

I pointed to the list I had handed him earlier. "Your supervisors are allowing the officers to enter our room. If I file a suit against the State, these people will be named...as well as you." The sense of injustice fueled my mouth with words of contempt.

The Chief glanced at the list. "Okay, Maggie. You and Bonnie will have the only keys."

As I was leaving, I turned. "Boys will be boys, Chief—but not in my world. Not anymore."

My fight didn't end there. The Chief had sent out a 24-bulletin 81-52 notice, which every officer and supervisor was required to read and sign, which stated the need for all male officers to refrain from entering the women's locker room. On the end of his memo, he used the word, "boys."

Well if you ever want to tick a man off, just call him a "boy." In reply to the Chief's 24-hour bulletin 81-52, an officer wrote in part the following response:

"You did not state what items were placed in the women's locker room or when. I would like to report that on the day shift only, I have observed no less than 7 non-department persons, a staff Officer, 3 watch commanders, and 4 line Officers in and around the construction area that was and now is the afore mentioned room in the past 2 weeks, none of whom, I believe, to be appropriately referred to as <u>BOYS.</u>

"Is this item an attempt to placate a few radical officers who might have caused this problem to further their own goals, or is it an attempt to alienate our women officers. Some of the men Officers would say, "I do not have a key to my locker room or shelves, or mirrors, or space to place my safety equipment, or new tile floor, or new paint job. I had thought that the United States Supreme Court had ruled discrimination, even in equal but separate facilities [sic], illegal under the Civil Rights Act. Where are all of these things for the men of this department?"

And in the end the memo reads:

"Although this memo was drafted and typed by me, I wish to express that the content is the feelings of a large portion of the department."

Of course, when I was handed the memo, my first thought was, "Just hire more women so we can be as crowded as you are!"

The memo confirmed my decision to move into a separate locker room and wondered again what took me so long. The memo was devastating to me. But it wasn't so much my misunderstanding of the men's' reaction to this change. It was more like my understanding of a direction I needed to take and was going to take.

Chapter Twenty-Three

1969

The sense of being alone wasn't new to me. Feeling isolated and rejected felt like friends—they were that familiar. During a good portion of my life, anyway—until I felt confident to overcome its obstacles and brave enough to fight back. By the time I left home at 18 years old, I was careless, reckless and on a self-destructive path. The violation and vulnerability of my youth would haunt me forever. The senselessness of not being protected as a child left me making questionable decisions as an adult.

1981

The women's hair regulation was changed to "neat and presentable." Poof, just like that.

My shift was about to begin when Tim contacted me in the fire stall.

"Don't do this, Maggie."

I had intentions of walking into roll call with a tight white T-shirt on that said "Never Underestimate the Power of a Woman." Ha! I was willing to take the heat for not being in uniform and at this point I didn't care. Along with the T-shirt, I let my hair down below my collar. I had won the change of hair policy but the men had to fight their own battle. They were still required to adhere to the military haircut. I found their anger that we won ludicrous. I laughed at the men's predicament. In the end, they used me to try and gain their goal. They used me in their own fight for relaxed hair regulations stating it was double standards because I could pin my hair up.

When the Chief reviewed their concerns, he stated, "Let them pin up their own hair."

I knew it was only a matter of time before the guys would win because now it was double standards. But, just this once, I wanted to feel the satisfaction of grinding a message into the Good Ole Boys Club.

Tim repeated his concern, "Don't do this, Maggie. It'll only get worse."

"What? You don't think I've earned this right to shove it in their faces?"

"They didn't make the rules. Just forget it."

Two weeks before Bonnie and I decided to fight the hair discrimination, Captain Edwards contacted me. "Maggie, I shouldn't be telling you this, but the guys just filed a complaint, using you as an example of double standards in the department."

That such conversations still existed regarding my hair was draining. I was exhausted about the whole ordeal.

"My hair is up, Captain Edwards! How could that possibly be a double standard?"

"Just make sure it stays up," he said.

The roll call buzzer for the day shift went off and I was still standing in the truck stall thinking about Tim's words. Maybe he was right. I dashed back to my locker room and put my uniform shirt on but I didn't pull up my hair. Compromise.

I was ending my day shift patrol in the vehicle and pulling into Station One to write my report. All I could think about was going home. Fighting for my rights was always draining but exhilarating at the same time. To be able to win the hair regulations was a big deal and I was proud to have made that change with Bonnie.

It was a sunny day after weeks of cloudy, rainy days and, as I stood in roll call, I visualized myself sitting on my back porch and having a beer. Tim and I had moved into a nice neighborhood. I was very happy living there and enjoyed all the neighbors. We had a healthy connection and often socialized. It was good to be friends with people who had different jobs.

I would live there for twenty-seven years.

Then I heard over the radio that an airplane had crashed and three men came running up to me, yelling, "There's been a crash at the lake!"

"Which one/"

"Lake Spenard, by the taxi canal hit Gull Island!"

I accelerated the patrol car and headed for the Lake Hood boat-house for the 85—horsepower jet engine rescue boat. It was fast. Plus, it had a drafting pump with a hose in case there was a fire.

I was the third to arrive at the boathouse. I slammed on my brakes and flew out of the patrol car. I raced to get my fire bunkers out of the trunk. I wasn't going to be left behind!

I had expected the other two officers to already have the boat going, but they couldn't get it started. Chuck Chamberlain was frustrated and close to panic.

"I can't get the boat started!"

He stood 6'2," considerably overweight. Wasn't there a weight-proportion-to-height requirement?

"Move!" I yelled at him.

I jumped into the boat and threw in my bunkers. I knew I had to jury-rig the gears to get the boat started. I grabbed the throttle and wiggled it a tad, then hit the starter. The boat roared to life. Man, that felt good. Chuck Chamberlain got into the boat and sat in the back. The other officer went back to the ramp, working as ramp captain. We had Lieutenant Nebgen coming from the other boathouse across the lakes.

The maintenance crew must have used the boat last because it was docked front-first into the boathouse and had to be backed out. The boats are supposed to be backed in for quick exit, in an emergency, like *now*.

I grabbed the radio. "Hood Tower, this is Rescue One. Request clearance from Boathouse One to the east-west taxi canal.

"Rescue One, you are cleared to proceed."

"Roger, Hood Tower."

I slammed the reverse throttle full bore—and immediately hit the boathouse! Boom! Thump!

I slammed the throttle forward. Boom! Thump! I hit the *front* of the boathouse! *I can't believe this.*

Finally clearing the boathouse in full reverse, I entered the waterway, whipped the boat around, hit full throttle forward and sped off. As I found control of my boat, I wondered what that 'thump' was as I lurched forward and backward.

The boat should be kicking up some ass about now, but it was sluggish. I turned around and there was Chuck flopping in the bottom of the boat like a fish out of water.

Now, I got it. Thump! Every time I had changed gears or hit the boathouse, he went flying with nothing to hold onto. I almost started to laugh.

We finally picked up speed. As I approached the canal and Gull Island, I slowed the boat but not enough – because when I hit the island, I almost flew over the steering wheel. Thump! Poor Chuck. I turned around. He was down again.

"You going to be okay, Chuck?"

He nodded wearily. "Yeah, yeah. Just go. I'll get there." He waved me off.

I took off running. The airplane had hit the island about fifty yards away. I didn't see a fire, so I left my bunkers in the boat. The island was named after all the seagulls that nested there, so I ran through the woods, opting to deal with spider webs rather than bird turds.

I was the first to the crash site and quickly assessed it. It was a small Cessna on floats with only two passengers who had already gotten out of the plane.

"We're okay," the man said helping his wife. "I think we broke one of our floats when we hit."

"Do you want the paramedics?" I asked.

"No, no, we're okay, really. Just embarrassed."

I turned my attention to the Lieutenant who had just arrived in the smaller boat from the Spenard Lake. "Have you seen Chuck?"

"Yes, around the corner picking bird crap off his coat." He smiled.

I cracked up. Poor Chuck hadn't taken the alternate route.

Since I was getting off duty, Lieutenant Nebgen excused me from the crash site and had another officer come out to write the report. I was glad, I preferred my back porch.

Chapter Twenty-Four

1962

At age eleven and in the sixth grade, I found another opportunity to try my hand at competing. I was intrigued with the game of marbles. The competition included a circle on the floor made with string. I knew the boys would try to shoot the marbles with as much force as they could muster, hoping to blast the center marbles into a million different directions. But I saw that the more force they used, the more the shooting cat-eye marble bounced and missed the center.

There was a marble competition at our school and all 600 students were invited to try out. I don't know how many kids actually did try out, but in the end there was only several boys and me. I was the only girl, and the boys didn't feel I was a threat.

My special shooting technique looked wimpy, but, by golly, it worked. Instead of trying to blast the center with force, I lay my hand flat and scooted it to the circle. Then I let go with all my thumb could take... and I eliminated the bounce!

The remaining boys in the competition began to copy me; antsy because I was winning.

When I walked out of school that day, with my marble trophy gripped in my hand, I walked home alone. I had thought the recognition would bring me friends, or at least someone to walk home with me. But it didn't.

Today, I proudly display that trophy in my office.

It sits alongside my weapon's proficiency trophy.

Maggie taken at the Police Academy, Sitka, Alaska by Andrea Jacobson.

1982

I soaked the sponge in soapy water and swashed it over the fire engine, then scrubbed the metal siding with a long wooden-handled brush.

Captain Grant shuffled up behind me. Although a doctor had told him in 1973 he'd never walk again without crutches after his car accident, Donald Grant had abandoned those months ago and his legs were mending. No more clinking, click, click, click of the aluminum. I was hoping without his crutches his disposition would improve. I knew he was often in pain from the nerve damage in his legs.

"Well, I've got good news or bad news, Maggie, depending on how you look at it."

I arched my eyebrows in anticipation. I could handle just about anything at this time in my life. "What is it?"

"You're going to the police academy in Sitka."

I yelled, "When? When? When?"

He smiled, I guess that means it's good news?"

"Oh, yeah, Captain. Just tell me when."

"Two weeks. The Chief has a list of things you need to take."

Standing in front of the Chief in his office in the Terminal Building, he handed me the list of items to take. Mostly rain gear. Sitka receives between 86 – 92 inches of rainfall a year.

"Do I need a physical before I go?" I asked the Chief.

"No, no you don't. Don't worry about it."

At the time, his words didn't mean anything. "Don't worry about it." That's what he said.

Seven years after my hire date, I arrived at the Public Safety Training Academy, (run by the Alaska State Troopers), in May, 1982. I would celebrate my thirty-first birthday during this academy.

Sitka, Alaska is a small fishing village on the southeast coast of Alaska. The coastal community was the original capital of the Territory of Alaska when it was purchased from the Russians. Tucked alongside a scenic forest, it has a wealth of Russian and Tlingit Indian history.

Walking off the Boeing 727 airplane, I counted six other recruits that had shared the plane ride. Standing inside the small Terminal Building, we were met by First Sergeant Jenkins. His Alaska State Trooper hat, similar to the old cavalry, was dark blue. The hat was tipped forward just above his dark eyebrows. The gold stripe that ran down the outside of his trousers was bright against the dark blue pants. His black, shiny shoes glistened even under the artificial light. He stood at 'parade rest' with his hands behind his back, legs twelve inches apart. He wasn't smiling.

"Get your gear, let's go!" There was a sense of impatience in his voice.

We scrambled to collect our belongings in the baggage area and hauled them outside to the waiting bus that would take us to the academy. We were the first seven of twenty-two recruits to arrive.

The academy building was two-stories in which all the male recruits would be housed on the upper level. There were two of us women and we shared a room downstairs.

My roommate was from Ketchikan, Alaska, not far from Sitka. We introduced ourselves and unpacked. Andrea had long, straight blond hair that dropped below her waist. Her light blue eyes and straight white teeth smiled as she shook my hand.

"Are you a cop?" I inquired.

"No, actually, I'm not. I put in for a position of police officer in Ketchikan and they sent me to this academy. I think they're trying to tell me 'Don't bother.' I'm actually a clerk with the city."

"Wow," I said, "Sounds like my department!"

As we gathered in the Day Room of the upper level of the building that evening, we were given the rules and expectations. The Alaska State Troopers ran the six-week academy. Twenty-two of us came from varying police agencies from around the state. The three of us from the Anchorage Airport were the only state officers; the remaining were city officers.

Kenny Mitchell and Tennison were the other two from my department. Kenny had been with the Department for four years and Tennison was a true rookie. He had just been hired.

During the academy he asked to leave to see his son graduate from high school. I was disgusted he would give up his spot in a police academy for that reason. Big deal his son is graduating.

I had never had a child and was only recently married. But I now understand his drive and I think that was the bravest act to leave a training to see your child graduate. As a mother years from that day—I applaud you as a father. I would have left, too, to see my kids graduate.

The first evening wound down and I crawled onto the thin, hard mattress of the lower bunk. The rooms were small, although there were two sets of bunk beds and two desks with two small closets. According to instructions given earlier, all our uniforms would be precisely hung in one direction, shoes neatly placed on the bottom, ready for inspection. Our beds would be made in a military fashion, bedspread so tightly tucked under the mattress, you could see the mattress seam. And, like the military, you could flip a quarter in the air and it would bounce from the unyielding material stretched to its limits.

Early the next morning after making our bunks and dressing for the day, my roommate, Andrea, and I were chatting when a knock on the door turned our attention. When I opened the door, First Sergeant Jenkins came in with another male trooper.

"Officer Foster!" Sergeant Jenkins yelled at me. "Why did it take you seven years to get here?"

I snapped to attention, face forward and blurted out, "Poor administration, sir!"

Andrea stood next to me.

He scoffed, walked to my bunk and ripped it apart and threw the mattress to the floor. "It's not right, Foster. Fix it!"

Chapter Twenty-Four

I scrambled to his demands. "Yes, sir!"

Our daily routine began at five in the morning, meeting in the lobby at 5:30, stretching for 30 minutes then a one-mile run around the scenic Totem Park

After the run (I threw up the first day trying to stay close to the guys), we would shower and run to breakfast, which was located, another half mile down a trail to the local college. Classroom lectures were given in the morning until noon. After lunch, we practiced physical techniques such as felony stops, pursuit driving, weapons training, search and seizure, use of physical restraints, and arrest procedures.

The new Alaska Criminal Code had recently been implemented and our laws had changed. Introductions to the new laws were a significant part of our mornings. Before the laws changed, a domestic violence victim would have to file a complaint and have the spouse arrested. The retribution and fear that the victim having the perpetrator arrested could torch more violence. The law changed putting the power into the police hands. The police could determine probable cause to arrest then they could make the arrest. It was one of the best laws I remember that made a positive change for victims of domestic violence. It took the decision out of the hands of the victim.

Homework was issued every night and all lectures concluded with a written test. Enough to keep us on our toes and alert.

On a rainy afternoon we gathered along the forest's edge where we were practicing felony stops. There were two officers in each of two patrol cars and emergency vehicles with red lights and sirens, which stopped a van from going in a wooded area. Initially, I was in the class that stood back and observed. The officers stepped out of their cars, with guns drawn toward the van, and declared specific orders: "With your left hand, take the keys out of the ignition and throw them out the window. Then exit the vehicle, using your right hand to open the door."

Suddenly, a jogger came running out of the woods directly into the scenario, causing a shift in attention and all guns pointed at him.

The officers yelled, "Get down! Get down! Face the ground!"

The jogger hesitated, which made it look real to us. Then he went white.

The officers yelled again, "Get down! Face the ground! Put your hands behind your head!"

Without question, the man hit the ground. Two officers approached him. The other two watched the driver exit the van. The jogger was handcuffed while trying to explain himself. We all believed this was part of the scenario: teaching us to never listen to excuses, to sift out the facts after everyone is safe.

The sergeant who evaluated us pointed to the jogger. "Who's this guy?"

A rookie meekly answered, "He came running out in front of the van, sir."

"He's not a part of any set up I'm aware of. Take the handcuffs off him, he ordered "and apologize."

Unknowingly, we must have scared the living day lights outta that guy!

Our lives had started to settle down some and became routine. The days rolled by quickly and soon we entered our third week in the academy.

As we gathered in the classroom for the morning lecture, the Sergeant, a dark-haired, handsome young man announced our lecturer was a professor from the University of Alaska in Fairbanks. The topic: Multi-Culture Awareness.

As I was trying to resolve exactly what multi-culture awareness was, Sergeant Lewis said, "Maggie, I see you don't have a physical on file. You will be excused from this academy until you get one. You're dismissed!"

The blood drained from my face as I made no effort to leave. Did I hear him correctly? How was I supposed to get to a doctor? WHAT doctor? What transportation? What doctor could take me on the spur of the moment?

Sergeant Lewis, seeing I wasn't moving, walked up the elevated rows of the classroom and stood beside me.

He handed me the keys to the school bus that the academy used. "Take these, Maggie. You're gonna have to find a doctor, get a physical and get back here ASAP. Check with the secretary out front, she might be able to help you find a doctor."

My world was crashing. I was fragmented, drowning in an endless whirlpool. Unable to understand why this happened.

Slowly I rose and left the classroom thinking, *How am I supposed to drive a school bus?*

The secretary, a very nice older lady with dark-rimmed large glasses and pink lipstick, sat behind the open window. Her bony fingers ran through the phone book as she said, "We don't have too many doctors, you know. Hopefully, you won't have a problem." She stopped at an advertisement then began to dial. "We'll pitch a good story; maybe he'll take pity."

I needed pity. My heart was racing.

The secretary hung up the black phone and said, "He can take you in an hour." She wrote the address down, then explained to me how to get there.

My hands were sweaty holding onto the bus keys. I've never driven a bus before. It was clutch. Thank goodness I knew how to drive a manual shift.

Raining. Always raining. I stepped up into the driver's side and took a deep breath. *How did this happen?* I was nervous about missing the lecture. All lectures had tests either that day or the next morning.

I snaked my way through the small town of Sitka and found the doctor's office. *How do you park a school bus?* I left it on the edge of the lot, probably a non-parking area.

The doctor, a man in his fifties, white hair and liquid blue eyes, entered the dressing area. I had filled out all the paperwork and anxiously waited for this to be over. I sat on the edge of the gurney, naked under the pale blue and white robe.

When the doctor was finished, he gave me a written report to give to the sergeant. I didn't read it until I left. Scribbled were words that only another doctor should see, describing my private parts.

As I entered the classroom, the recruits were taking the test for Multi-Culture Awareness. Making eye contact with the sergeant, my mind raced whether to give him the note. My privacy disintegrated. I flushed with embarrassment and humility.

Sergeant Lewis took the note without looking at it and handed me the test. "You got ten minutes."

I sat down and watched him open the note. He made no comment or facial expressions. He merely folded it back.

Passed my physical.

I flunked the test. Flunking a test will cause discharge from the academy. If I flunked the academy, I would be dismissed from my job. I would be allowed to take the test two more times. After that, bon voyage!

On the second day, I flunked it again.

Before the third try, I was contacted by one of the recruits who had been a teacher. "Maggie," he started out, "I'm going to teach you how to take a test without knowing the subject."

He had my full attention. His name was Chris and was a police officer in Kake, a small village on the southeast coast of Alaska. Chris winked at me and with his ready smile and calm demeanor, took my hand and looked in my eyes. "Don't worry. You'll get through this. I didn't understand the class or the test." Reassuring in a pathetic way.

On the third day I sat in the classroom alone and took the test.

I passed. And that crisis was over.

And the next one began.

I called Tim at home to check in. The immediate silence that followed my greeting did not prepare me for his accusations.

His voice was flat. "What happened on your last test? Did you flunk it?"

Guarded and surprised by the force of his words, I simply replied, "I passed the test, Tim. What's your concern?"

"It makes you look bad! They (*whoever they were, I wasn't privileged to know*) are thinking you're not going to make it, an embarrassment!"

I concluded the telephone call quickly, too confused to even ask questions. *Who even told them I flunked?* If the Department couldn't get me to quit, maybe they were looking to get me fired. I was angry with Tim for not supporting me. And for not seeing the injustice that I was told I didn't have to have a physical.

To ease my stress, I ran. I ran alone after dinner in the early evenings. The summer days were long and the sun didn't set until after 10:00 at night. My feet would pound the soft, moist ground of the trail that meandered around the historical totem poles. Whispers of ancestral stories of the Indians and Russians flowed through the evening dew. As I rounded the outer edge of the forest that met the sea, I left the earthy smells of nature.

I could hear the water lapping against the trail's edge before I cleared the forest. Once in the open, the salt of the sea permeated the air, unfastening a new world.

Wrestling was another physical task we had to perform. I was paired up with a man, but not the biggest man, in the academy. We sat back to back, interlaced our arms and the whistle blew. The object was to get my opponent off the mat we were sitting on.

An automatic response would be to stand and that's what I figured he would do. And he did. I kept my weight low and easily flipped him off the mat! I think I was as surprised as he was. One round for the girl.

A moment later standing with my pride beaming in my conquest to kick ass, Jim Norton jumped me from behind. Jim was a professional football player turned cop. He worked in Juneau, our capital. He was the largest and strongest man in the class.

Coming from behind me, his large arms grabbed me across my chest and he jokingly said, "Okay, Maggie, what are you going to do when someone MY size gets you?"

The entire class and instructors waited for my answer.

Because Jim hadn't pinned my lower arms down, I shifted my hips to the side, and then smacked him in the balls with my fist. He went down like lead.

The class was laughing and First Sergeant Jenkins asked, "So, Norton, what are you going to do when a gal Maggie's size gets a hold of you?" More laughter.

Other practical testing included "pursuit driving" in which I placed second to the last! The instructor had us drive at a high rate of speed, then at the last split second, he would yell "right, left or center" and you would have to turn your vehicle in that direction, staying between the cones. I kept anticipating, and slowing up, waiting for the instructions. I sucked.

Then there was the weapons qualification. During the early practice, we all had the opportunity to shoot the police proficiency course or PPC. We were required to shoot the course once to see if we needed additional practice. A qualifying score of seventy percent was the minimum score.

The day I practiced, I dropped six rounds onto the ground – nervous maybe.

The sergeant yelled at me, "Pick them up! You only have so much time." Then, for some reason, he added, "Never mind, just pick them up and shoot. Okay, Maggie?"

So I did and before I could reload all of them he called the time. "That's it, no more time!"

"What? You said 'Just do it.' You weren't timing me, were you?"

"No, no, I never said that." He scored it—seventy percent. "You need more practice, Maggie. Let me know, I'll help you out." I glared at him with contempt.

A fellow officer from the airport and I were walking on the lower level of the academy where various awards for all the practical testing were displayed. In the middle of the case was the weapons qualification trophy.

"What do you shoot, Kenny?"

"Maybe high 80s, low 90s, why?"

"Just checking out my competition. Who do you suppose can beat me on the weapons qualifications?"

Kenny and I had worked together five years and he knew I earned a master's patch that was sewn on my left sleeve cuff on my uniform. For me to wear the patch, I would have to qualify with 95 percent or higher. I was very proud of it.

"Nobody," he said. "I think you've got a chance, Maggie. Really."

I didn't want to get my hopes up. There were many different departments attending the academy, and different guns were involved. I carried a Smith and Wesson .38-caliber Model 15, a relatively small gun, but I was accurate. And I was familiar with the PPC course.

I looked at the trophy and pronounced, "That's mine, Kenny. I'm going to win that."

The day of the competition, I stood poised among my peers. I was about to make history and I knew it. When the whistle sounded to start, I fired and blew the center right out of the target.

"Did you lose any rounds, Maggie?" The sergeant asked, scrutinizing my target.

"No, sir; I didn't throw any." My score, 98.6.

I watched his reaction and knew I had a good chance of placing first in this competition. I didn't realize that the top gun in the history of the academy of 98.7.

"Not bad," he mumbled as he walked away to score the other targets.

If I placed first, I would be the first woman in the history of the academy to do so. Winning this trophy would give me the honor of having my name on the plaque for weapons proficiency and the only woman whose name was displayed in the hallway of the academy.

I would have to wait a week for graduation day to know who placed first. Rumors flew regarding my standing on the weapons qualification and I tried to keep my hopes under control. Guys were talking and congratulating me but still, it wasn't official. There was a sinking feeling that one other recruit had a realistic chance to out-score me. And he wasn't talking.

As I stood in line for graduation, I had my full police uniform on with all the accolades, which included the master's patch for weapons qualification that I had previously earned and maintained.

The recruit in front of me turned. "Maggie, is this your police uniform?" I had been wearing my fire uniform the entire time at the academy because it was more comfortable. And our police uniforms had to be dry-cleaned. I knew I could get away with it because our patch on our fire uniforms said "Airport Police." I was caught.

"Yes. I fudged a little. This is actually my police uniform. Don't tell my captain!" I laughed out loud. I was nervous.

Referring to the weapons trophy, the recruit said, "You deserve this, Maggie… and you deserve the honor of being the first woman to qualify number one."

I dismissed his compliment. I didn't really know yet if I had won.

Anxiously I sat there among my peers, waiting for the announcement. Spouses and children sat behind us.

My closest competition sat beside me. As they began to announce the recipient of the trophy for firearms proficiency, he leaned over. "You won it, Maggie. It's yours. Congratulations."

"… in the history of the academy," said the announcer, "there has never been a woman achieve this award. I proudly present to you Margaret Foster."

That night I called Captain Grant at his house. Not Tim. Not my Mom. Not my best friend. Captain Grant. I needed to know he was proud of me.

"Hello?"

"Hi, it's me, Captain Grant." I started slow but my edge of excitement was pushing me to continue.

"Hi, Maggie. What's up?"

Our relationship had improved over the years. "Well…" I was embarrassed about bragging but I was sure this would seal his respect. "I qualified number one in weapon's proficiency. First woman in the history of the academy." I waited anxiously for his response.

"I knew you could do it. That's good. I'm proud of you."

And that sealed it. It took seven years.

When my plane landed in Anchorage I searched for Tim in the crowd. When I did find him, he turned away and walked several feet ahead.

In the car, I held onto my weapon's proficiency trophy while Tim complained. "You know that test you flunked is in your personnel file. You almost didn't make it, Maggie."

Chapter Twenty-Five

Thanksgiving at fire station one.
Jovanovich, Fleming, Rayfield and Maggie.

1982

Back from the academy, I was excited to put into action what I had learned. Our little airport was busy with police calls: an attempted murder where a young oriental man had sliced another man's throat with a machete; a dead body in the trunk of a car; traffic accidents with fatalities; numerous drug and weapons confiscated at the screening gates; fights; and lots of drunks. The Alaska pipeline was in full swing bringing thousands more through our terminal. Enough to keep me on my toes. I loved it.

I worked most of the holidays because they never landed on my days off. And when they did, I volunteered to work it for those who had families. I loved organizing the holidays in the station. Christmas, Thanksgiving. I'd have everyone bring a dish and invite their families for Thanksgiving. Those who worked would have a chance to be with their families and love ones. I found happiness in that vicariously. I didn't have a family or married when I began the rituals. But after I did have a family, those Holidays in the fire station were very rewarding, especially the school field trips. I was so enthusiastic and involved I became the "master" of field trips. One teacher told me, "This is the best field trip I've ever been on." Which is quite the kudo because the school district never considered the airport fire station as an educational tool.

It was mid-winter, 1982. Entering the fire station for duty, the Dispatcher contacted me through the intercom.

"Maggie, as soon as you finish roll call, report to South Air Park."

"Got it." I said as I punched my time card.

Tim had already briefed me; he had called me at home mid-morning. "We have a situation where a man commandeered a Lear Jet at South Air Park. Troopers are here. You're scheduled for Ramp Captain this afternoon."

"Do you want me to come in early?"

"No, we have enough people. F.B.I. is here, too." Then he continued, "The guy is alone but he's got a gun. He's been hold up in there for several hours already."

"Any hostages or injuries?"

"No. I just wanted to let you know. I gotta go."

"Okay, see ya."

The information soaked in while standing next to my phone, I let out a slow breath and wondered how my evening was going to end?

During roll call, the Watch Commander, Lieutenant McCurley ordered, "Maggie, take a ladder to South Air Park. Stay over there. We need a liaison and you're it."

The Troopers and their Special Emergency Reaction Team (SERT) had been dispatched along with Airport Police and the FBI. The hijacker had come to the airport early to charter an airplane to Salt Lake City. He wanted to meet the leader of the Mormon Church and resolve personal issues. He was a skilled engineer but had been fired from his job three years before and his life had taken a spiral downward. He had a psychiatric history and a fascination with guns.

When he had arrived at the ticket counter, the airline clerk saw the gun and an ice-pick under his coat. She called the cops.

I arrived at the small terminal building and there were a myriad of police in the area. It was just after 4:00 in the afternoon.

The head of the Trooper's SERT was George Pollitt, a seasoned and tough cop. His presence commanded respect.

We waited during the long negotiations.

The plane had been moved from the hanger to the apron area at the request of the hijacker. There was a trooper lying on his back under the jet listening and communicating with Pollitt. I imagined the young trooper lying on the cold winter ground, waiting, listening. Preparing himself for the worst.

When I saw that Pollitt had a break in communications, I introduced myself to him. "I was told to bring a ladder."

"Yeah, forget that; we don't need it."

I think that was the extent of our conversation. From that point forward, I listened and watched.

I could see the airplane through the large windows until darkness came. Then I eased myself through the room of officers to see better. As I did so, I felt exposed knowing the man had a gun and I was at the window. I stepped back.

How long would this last? I wondered. The original call had come in eleven hours before.

Six o'clock rolled around. I was standing among the FBI and troopers when we heard a muffled shot.

Then the radios burst with information and the trooper underneath the plane whispered into his radio. He said everything was quiet.

We waited. Nothing else happened. Finally the troopers pulled a staircase to the front of the plane, climbed up and looked in. The hijacker was in the second seat back, slumped over, not moving. He was dead.

Chapter Twenty-Six

1968

I lay in the bed that my brother, Benji, used to sleep in down-stairs in our home. I had taken over his old bedroom but the door didn't lock and even at age 17, that was a concern. I didn't trust my parents to ever come to my room for any reason.

That evening, like most, was filled with drinking, argu-ments, accusations, and damage. You could hear it and I couldn't get rid of it.

So when I heard my dad's voice as he started to open the door to my safety, I literally launched myself from my lying position to kick closed the partially open door that my dad had opened.

In doing so, the door slammed against his face and broke his nose. Blood everywhere. He staggered backwards, and then fell on his butt holding his nose.

I tried to comfort him.

1982

This is me, seven months pregnant, standing beside Engine 2 Heavy, largest crash truck in the world. It carries 6,000 gallons of water and 515 gallons of light-water. From the upper turret, it can disperse 800 gallons a minute from a single discharge rate and 1,800 gallons a minute on a dual discharge rate. So if you approach a fire and use a dual discharge rate, you will have just over three minutes before you empty your entire 6,000 gallons.

I assisted and directed the development of the first Field Training Program (FTO) for the airport police and fire department and became one of the first FTOs (Field Training Officer). I taught new recruits how to drive and operate this truck.

Four months after the hijacking on Christmas Eve, 1982, the nurse called me at home. "Would you like to know the results of your pregnancy test?"

Tim was upstairs watching television. I cupped the phone to mute my voice. "Yes! Yes! Yes!"

"It's positive. Merry Christmas."

Two simple words: "It's positive." Then my life moved onto something more valuable.

It didn't put my current fight with the State, or controversies to come, on hold. But it did put a new perspective in my life. And that was more powerful than any job or agenda or man or anything in my life. My child meant everything. And I was willing to sacrifice anything/everything for this child.

"You just made this the best Christmas of my life," I whispered back.

As I put down the phone, closing the conversation, I felt ecstatic, like the world was about to get much better. I knew it! I had taken two pregnancy home-tests and they were negative so I took a blood test through my doctor. Positive! There was no mistaking the definite change in my body, my emotions, my feelings, and now my future.

It would be Christmas Day that I would tell Tim.

I handed him the card that I placed between the bows of our Christmas tree.

"Here's the last present," I said watching him open the card.

I wrote, "You cannot give me anything more than the gift of life. Merry Christmas. You're going to be a father."

Tim drew me to him and held me tightly as he whispered, "I love you."

Life was good.

I would remain on the midnight shift at work through the next three months; then I would tell my Chief. Although I wanted to tell the world, Tim asked me to keep it quiet the first three months. Easy for a man to say. Very difficult for a woman, for me, because I was so happy and so sick. Not throwing up sick, just tired, exhausted, and always on the verge of throwing up. And who wants a gun belt on at this point, wrapped tightly around the waist.

I would be the first woman pregnant in the department so who knew what was going to happen.

The following February, just short of three-months pregnant, I was on the midnight shift at Fire Station One. I was alone in the kitchen, resting my feet up on the table, leaning back with my fingers interlaced behind my head, concentrating on not getting sick. I had loosened my pant belt and unhooked my pants. I couldn't stand anything tight – I couldn't stand anything touching me.

I was nodding off when a voice over the loud speaker suddenly bellowed, "Maggie, you back there?"

My dream state busted with a rapid heartbeat that almost threw me into convulsions. "Yeah! You scared the crap out of me." My legs came off the table with a thud as I leaned over the table hiding my head into my folded arms. I didn't want to hear what was coming.

"Get your gun belt on. You're going up to the terminal. They've got a problem with a woman up there."

Over the years, women came and went from our department and currently there were three of us. "Send Skyes. She's the ramp captain. I'm working fire. Tell her to do it!" I was so demanding. I didn't want to move. I was still trying to control my heartbeats, which were pounding against my chest.

"She can't handle this, Maggie. Get your gear on and get up there. The woman is a fighter. It took several men to get her down before when cops were called.

Before? I sighed and reluctantly eased myself out of the chair. This would be a good time to tell them I was pregnant. Let me go home, go to bed, nurture my delicate state.

Instead, I went to my locker and put on my gun belt. It was snug around my waist. The last thing I wanted was to be cinched up tight. Maybe I could wear it bandit style, across my shoulders? Or low on my hips, like the cowboys, strapped to a leg?

"Okay!" I yelled to the intercom. "I'm ready. Who's taking me up?"

"Take a patrol car, Maggie, and hurry. They've got a real problem up there."

Good grief! Couldn't anyone drive me?

At the terminal building, the patrol car idled in the cold winter night. In the rearview mirror, I watched the exhaust rise before I slowly exited the vehicle and entered the Terminal Building from the lower level. Two male officers, a young woman about six-months pregnant, and her husband were standing outside the women's bathroom.

"What's going on?" I asked, trying to muster concern.

The young woman came to me. "That's my mom in there." She pointed to the bathroom. "We're committing her to the Alaska Psychiatric Institute (API). *Suddenly, I feel sorry for her. It's got to be hard.*

"Okay, but what's the problem?"

She tightly held onto her husband's hand as she explained, "She won't come out." Her slender hand drew through her dark hair in exasperation. "She doesn't have any clothes on."

I sucked in a deep breath and let it out slowly. "I hear she's a fighter. Is that true?"

Tears formed in a pool around the girl's eyes. "Yeah. That might be a problem."

Waves of nausea passed through me, and I wondered what I was doing here. "All right then, I'll go in."

The mother was very large and naked. She had taken off all her clothes, and placed them in four different sinks in the bathroom. Water was overflowing.

I carefully approached her and turned off all the running water in each sink. Then I worked my way closer to her and asked if she would put on some clothes. Her response was incoherent so negotiating was out, and I was too sick to force her.

I walked out to my young partner. "Go get a blanket, Justin. She's naked."

He brought a wool blanket from the First Aid room around the corner and followed me back into the bathroom.

I told the woman I would be putting the blanket around her and handcuffing her. I turned to Justin. His eyes were closed and held out the blanket.

I grabbed the blanket. "Geeze, Justin. Open your eyes. Put the blanket around her." I threw it back to him.

Flushed with embarrassment, he wrapped the blanket around the woman. I was sorry I had been short with him. I needed this night to be over.

We brought her out of the bathroom and to her daughter, then I radioed in. "Dispatch, I'm finished with this situation. I'll be returning to Station One." I would not even sweep the floor at the end of this shift.

"Negative, 602 Alpha. You're transporting to API."

Oh, this was not good. It was crazy to think I could still work the midnight shift.

Everyone was looking at me, so I tried to be calm. *Okay, I thought, I can do this. I can do this.*

I told Justin to get shoes on the woman and take her to my patrol car. He sized up the situation. The woman was agitated, moving side to side, with the blanket barely covering her.

"Just get her in the car, "I said to him impatiently.

We put her in the back seat. He drove and I tried not to think of throwing up.

At the psychiatric hospital, we managed to get the woman out of the car and down the hallway. She struggled with us the entire time. Her daughter and the husband joined us in the admitting room. The staff member asked if she had any medical problems.

The woman lit up with excitement. "Got diabetes, I do!"

The nurse looked at Justin and me. "Does she?"

"I don't know," I said.

I looked to the daughter, who nodded and said, "She has some problems, yes."

So, the nurse said, "You have to take her to the hospital to clear her for booking back here at API.

"What? I thought this was a hospital?"

The nurse shook her head. "No. You have to clear her first at a hospital." I should have called in sick for the next nine months. Was I going to make it through this night?

Annoyed, I curtly asked, "Well, can we at least get some clothes on her?"

"Sure. We have some stuff here she can wear."

With the help of three staff members, Justin and I managed to clothe the woman and put soft slippers on her feet. We transported her to the emergency room at the local hospital while her daughter and husband waited at API.

She fought Justin and me all the way down the hall to the ER. When we finally sat her down, she started screaming and wouldn't stop. I was worn out. She went on and on and on, and my patience was running out. Everyone in the ER was staring at us.

A doctor finally escorted us to a room, but the woman continued screaming. Justin had gone to get a cup of coffee and clear his ears. I was alone with the woman when a doctor came down the hall. I barely heard what he said.

"What did you say, sir?"

"Can't you keep her quiet?" he asked in a raised voice.

I looked him in the eye. "Sure, I can. You got some of that surgical tape or duck tape I can put across her mouth?"

"You can't do that," he said aghast.

"Yes, sir. I guess you got your answer."

He turned on his heels with disapproval. *Welcome to my world, doc.*

I'd had enough of Mrs. Screamer. I suddenly turned, grabbed her by the mouth, and forced her down onto her back on the table. I put my face right up close to hers. "Shut up! Do you hear me? Shut up! Just shut up!"

I felt a grinding sensation and heard a crunching sound inside her mouth. *Uh, oh, did I break her jaw?*

I pulled her forward and let loose my grip. She spit out a set of dentures into my hand, uppers and lowers. Repelled, I jerked back.

She started yelling. "Better wash your hands! Better wash your hands!"

Justin returned at the moment of my humility. "Maggie, what's that in your hand?"

My heavy breathing signaled me to be calm. "Nothing," I whispered. "Absolutely nothing." I put the dentures on the table.

At the end of my three full months of pregnancy, I left the graveyard duty when my shift ended and drove to the Chief's office. The graveyard shift had tasked my limits.

"What's up, Maggie?" he asked from his power chair. His Boston accent echoed in my ears.

"I'm pregnant, Chief. Three months."

He swiveled in his chair, his fingers steeple. "Well, that's good, Maggie. We'll put you on light duty, Dispatch, starting tomorrow. That's good. You should have two. You should have two kids."

"Okay," I simply said. I was too tired to say anything else. It had been a long three months.

Captain Grant insisted that I maintain a uniform throughout the pregnancy, although he was liberal in letting me design what I felt appropriate as long as it passed required inspections.

Only occasionally did someone make a derogatory comment, such as, "So, are you going to quit this job, or be a part-time mother?"

I faced him in the kitchen of the fire station. "I guess that makes you a part-time father, huh?"

For the most part, during the months of my pregnancy the men treated me like royalty. I was changing before their eyes. I heard their own stories of their first children, making me feel connected in some way. I became someone they could protect. I was the woman and I knew, basically, they were proud of me. They brought me ice cream, complimented me on my new uniform and told me I "glowed"—which I did.

Chapter Twenty-Seven

Sometimes

The smell of bacon and potatoes and eggs in a black cast iron skillet always had our attention, although reserved. It was Sunday and dad was cooking like he did ever Sunday.

Some days my parents would be sober. And the strength of that joy held us together as a family. But it was nothing more than a tease; a reason to hold on and wait, anticipating another day when the ice beneath our feet would crack.

1983

The Dispatch office was a separate building a few yards south of the fire station. Four months after I began full-time in Dispatch, I received several calls from the FAA and NTSB regarding a Reeve Aleutian Airlines' four-engine turbo-prop aircraft in possible trouble inbound from Cold Bay, Alaska on the Aleutian Chain. I was trying to make sense of the scattered information when a young Italian man about my age entered into the office unexpectedly.

"Hi, I'm James Michalangelo with the NTSB. We have an Electra with its number four-engine propeller severed from the wing. The propeller hit the fuselage. The pilot has lost almost all control of the aircraft. We have fifteen souls on board. ETA is approximately 1900 hours (7 p.m.). I'll be setting up here in Dispatch with you and taking all the national calls. You'll be getting a lot of those. Just forward them to me. Here, show me how this panel works."

He didn't even take a breath. I stared at him, dumbfounded. Had I asked him for his ID? Oh, yeah, he'd flashed it at about his fourth sentence.

"Okay," I said, recuperating. "My name is Maggie, by the way."

"Okay, Maggie. Nice to meet you. Your lieutenant briefed me." He shook my hand. He was still standing. His little black eyes darted back and forth, back and forth.

"Right, okay. Nice that they briefed *me*."

"I'm going to do that. I *just* did that. I'll stay with you. This is going to get hairy."

"I've gotta go pee." I said and stood.

He glanced down at my enlarged seven-month belly.

"I'm seven months pregnant," I said. "I have to go to the bathroom all the time. I just need a relief to do that."

I called for one over the intercom. The relief showed up and I headed to the door.

"Hey, I forgot to tell you," James Michalangeloe said.

I turned.

"Wherever this plane lands, it's going to crash."

My baby kicked.

"We're just not sure where, okay? We're trying to get them here to International. Better rescue."

I walked out, trying to process all the information. When I returned, I contacted Tim, my husband, who had been promoted to lieutenant and asked him to explain what was going on.

"Sure, that's Michelangelo. He's NTSB. He's good. Just work with him, Maggie. He knows what he's doing."

"That's it?" I asked.

"Yes. This is going to be complicated."

"Right." Some briefing.

The Dispatch board lit up like a Christmas tree. Michelangelo was right. Calls from all over the United States, CBS, NBC, and CNN. We sat side by side at two separate control panels and I transferred out-of-state calls to him.

There were various lines of communication at the Dispatch office: direct to the Anchorage Police, Anchorage Fire and Paramedics, and Anchorage Control Tower. When on duty as Dispatcher, I monitored all radio frequencies of the Control Tower and aircraft on the ground and approaching runways for landing.

Normal traffic squawked through the Dispatch board, and the pending airplane emergency ran through my mind. In my nine years with the Department, this would be one of the most intense situations… and I was pregnant.

To control routine traffic, I instructed all mobile police and fire units to transmit on the second frequency and use it for emergencies only.

As the Aleutian aircraft came closer to landing, I had all police units report to the fire station, get their fire gear, and attend the remaining fire trucks not already assigned. In addition I recalled all off-duty firefighters back to the station. With mutual aid, we had approximately eighty rescue people coordinated in various locations. It was going to be a long night.

As the night progressed, I thought about the passengers on board the aircraft. *Were they aware of the seriousness of their situation?* The propeller had collided with the fuselage and severed the manual controls of the airplane and there was a three-by-four-foot gash in the side of the plane. *How were they going to make it here? How could the pilot land the plane?* Also, the front landing gear had been physically cranked down, but they weren't sure it was locked and it could collapse on landing. *Were they all going to die?*

Three hours before the anticipated landing, James Michalangelo set me up with a Reeve Airlines Dispatcher, Richard Huff. He and I fixed a direct phone line between the two of us. Huff would receive information from the pilot, transfer it to me, and I would dispatch to our rescue personnel.

In addition, we studied "what if" scenarios such as "hot" landings (coming in too fast for a safe landing). I took the information I was given and transferred it to the Watch Commander, Tim. In turn, he positioned the fire trucks where he hoped they would best perform. Water rescue teams near Cook Inlet were placed in case the airplane hit short of the runway, as well as fire trucks near the terminal building since the pilot had no steering ability and we weren't sure where he would end up. The trucks were strategically located along the entire runway.

I had to pee again. At this point, my inability to control my bladder provided some humor to this very intense situation. Since most of the firefighters were all busy, I had to call a supervisor. Captain Grant had stayed over from his day shift to help out in this emergency, so he became my relief. I was glad. It was helpful to have someone I knew nearby. As I left Dispatch this time, I felt everyone's nervous tension. I especially worried for the people on the plane.

At 5:40 p.m., the pilot, James Gibson, transmitted over the emergency frequency to the Anchorage Tower, advising that the three remaining engines were locked and at cruise speed, so he would have to shut them down for landing, which would give him no control. When the propeller hit the fuselage, it cut all controls to the remaining engines. The engines were locked in place.

A plane with no hydraulics, no steering and no flap control. He would be coming in "hot" – too fast to land and stop safely by the end of the runway. He would have to use his air brakes. Runway Six-Right was 10,600-feet long. Could he do it?

At 7:14 p.m., the aircraft was on final approach and the "crash phone" (red phone from the tower to the Dispatch office) rang. I grabbed it, wrote down the information, and hung up. I dispatched the following:

"Attention all units. Attention all units. We have an Electra on final to Runway Six-Right. Fifteen souls on board, ten passengers and five crew members; 17,000 pounds of fuel, no hazardous materials. The aircraft has no steering ability and will approach 'hot.' The aircraft will be flanked by two C-130s. All units respond."

I hit the fire alarm and it blared. The baby kicked. All five fire stall doors rose and four fire trucks and a 4,000 gallon tanker exited.

Fire Station Two responded with a 6,000-gallon fire truck, the biggest in the world, nicknamed "The Hog." Red lights and sirens. Clear the way. Power and safety on the way.

I stood in Dispatch, wishing I could be out there with them. I felt the exhilaration that comes from being part of a rescue. There is something to say about being on the front line. The pride of being part of something that comes together to support safety, property, and life is hard to beat. No matter what position you work.

Kulis Air National Guard responded from the south side of the field, back-up. The paramedics were held short, waiting. The Anchorage Fire Department held short, waiting.

At 7:20 p.m., the aircraft made its approach, flanked by the two C-130s from Kulis Air National Guard. In Dispatch, I focused my binoculars westbound and watched the events unfold. He was coming in low and fast.

"He's too fast!" I blurted to Michelangelo. "He's not going to make it!"

Michelangelo had his binoculars fixed on the in-coming plane. "Come on, girl, you can make it."

Then the pilot gunned it. He couldn't land, and was going around, trying again.

The thirteen minutes from when he left the runway and came back around seemed like a lifetime. I was sure I was going to have the baby. When I lost sight of the plane as it fell below the horizon, I held my breath. I expected to see black rolling smoke of a fuel fire.

When the plane reappeared, I yelled. "There it is! Michelangelo turned my direction. "I see it!"

I crossed my fingers behind my back, praying, "Please, please let him land."

Richard Huff continued to relay information. "He's still coming in hot. He'll feather all three engines on final. They'll blow the emergency air brakes."

I dispatched the information: "Expect a fire."

Then the pilot landed... and the plane was hot. The tires locked and began to smoke.

Then he slowed. Gradually, he slowed, and the plane came to a halt in the ditch, veering off but not over.

Spectacular! Incredible! Improbable!

James Gibson, he did it, the Reeve Aleutian pilot.

The smoke developed into a fire in the main landing gear, Engine two covered the entire fuselage in light water to prevent its spread while the air guard extinguished the wheel fire.

I watched the impressive coordination among all the different rescue teams.

The rear emergency exit was deployed, and the passengers slid down the chute. Firemen received them and scooted them to vans to come to the terminal. No one needed the paramedics. The passengers were shaken but in good condition.

Richard Huff said, "Thank you for all your help."

"The thanks go to your pilot. You have the best pilots in the world." I said, "The best of the best." They flew the Aleutian Chain in the most adverse weather conditions anywhere.

James Gibson and the cockpit crew received the Presidential Commendation for Bravery, and he met the President of the United States. Gibson also received the Dadaelin Award, given for the highest level of safety performed by airline pilots.

I worked a week past my due date. I left work on Friday, and my son, Joshua Benjamin, was born that Sunday, August 7th, 1983. The men had placed bets on the due date and time. Their attention towards me was honorable and, again, a piece here and there of their acceptance of me had a positive impact on my outlook, even my decision to return to work.

I had enough sick leave accumulated to take three months off to care for my baby and bond. My life changed from career to motherhood and I became totally consumed in this new direction. And for the first time in my life, I found a piece of heaven.

Mother and son

Chapter Twenty-Eight

1968

My father's fist struck my face and cracked my jaw. I heard it before I felt the pain.

My dad was slender, medium height. Half his stomach had been cut out from a severe ulcer as a young man and he ate like a bird. On a day of sobriety or maybe before he became drunk, he seemed like a decent person but distant. I never did know who he was. It was an era where kids were seen and not heard.

I was sixteen. The force of the blow sent me sideways onto my hands and knees. He was drunk and was trying to kill my parakeet, Elvis—named after The King. The bird was sick and making too much noise for my dad who sat next to the cage with his whiskey and cigarettes. He got up, grabbed the cage from its wall mount and started swinging it around, banging the bird inside against the walls. I was in the kitchen when I heard the noise and without hesitation ran to the swinging cage and tried to grab it from the grips of my dad. I was blind sided with the blow. I never saw it coming nor expected a strike to my face. Stunned by the punch, it took me a second to realize I had, in fact, retrieved the cage as it landed next to me with my hand clinched to it. I got up without looking back and ran with my bird to the only room upstairs in the house that locked.

1983

Maggie next to Engine 3 during the DC-10 crash.
Dale Falk in the truck and Charles Gilman on the handline.
Photo taken by John Bennett

Christmas was two days away. I had just started working again. The decision to return to work was difficult. It was hard to leave my infant. My time with my baby was so rewarding. I wasn't sure what caused me to return to work. I certainly had toyed with the idea of staying home. But maybe my need for independence drove me back to a career I loved as much as staying home. Could I have both? It was 1983 when women were making choices to stay at work. The whole issue of childcare was disconcerting: how do you leave the precious love of your infant in the hands of strangers? I had lucked out when Bob Leger said his wife could babysit.

Joshua cuddled his infant head against my neck as I held him close. I had finally gotten him to sleep. His little body was relaxed and I rocked him softly as I floated around the kitchen. I was expecting my mother and brother to show up for a visit and was planning a large meal. Amidst the preparations, my thoughts slipped to a cool stream on a sunlit mountain.

Joshua's presence was soothing to me. I was exhausted from trying to wean him and was between the stages of nursing and trying to get him to use a bottle.

Now that Tim and I were married and still within the five-mile radius to receive a home alarm in case of a recall, we had placed the unit in our bedroom where we could hear emergency orders in the middle of the night. Suddenly the home-alarm went off in the bedroom down the hallway. I rushed to it with Joshua in my arms. 2:10 in the afternoon, December 23, 1983.

"All off-duty firefighters return to work," the Dispatcher announced. "We have a possible DC-10 collision with a 747."

Joshua started crying, which intensified my stress. Still holding him, I ran in circles. *What did I just hear? How many people? Four hundred? Get a grip!*

I called my baby sitter, Clyda, Bob Leger's wife. Joshua continued screaming as I held him. When she told me Bob was asleep, I yelled, "Get him up! There's a recall!"

"Hello?" Bob's voice was thick with sleep.

"Wake up, Bob! Did you hear the recall?"

"I heard something about the training pits. I didn't know it was real. Thought it was training."

"It's real, Bob. Can Clyda baby-sit?"

"Yeah. Bring him and pick me up, would ya?"

"On my way!"

I slammed the receiver down without saying goodbye and grabbed the baby bottles and formula. Then the doorbell rang and I bounded down the stairs. I flung open the door, and there was my mother and brother.

"They just had a crash at the airport," I said breathlessly. "I have to go. I have to go. Can you watch Joshua?"

"Yes, yes. Just go."

My mom waved me off and I handed her my little guy. My mind was racing in a million different directions, thinking about casualties, bodies. I ran outside with the sound of my wailing baby following in my ears and the guilt in leaving him aching in my heart.

The dense fog and icy roads made driving slow and tricky. Speed was necessary but nearly impossible. I needed to calm down, but I was desperate to get to the airport. I felt a powerful force driving me—something I couldn't explain—like the feeling of being needed. A sense of responsibility.

By the time I got to Bob's house he had already left, and I told Clyda my mom had Joshua.

When I arrived at the fire station, the city fire and police departments had already begun to provide mutual aid. People were everywhere: city cops, medics, city fire, NTSB, FAA, maintenance people, off-duty and on-duty crash/rescue fire-fighters and the press.

I quickly changed into my fire gear and, along with three other firefighters, crammed myself into the back seat of a patrol car. The fog and massive smoke from the crash site were intensely thick. We could only see a few feet ahead.

We reported to the command vehicles for instructions. Lieutenant Tim Foster was directing and pairing us up and assigning trucks. He partnered me with Dale Falk on Engine Three.

Despite all the excitement, Tim took me aside. "Where's Joshua?"

"He's with my mom. He's okay."

"All right. You and Falk go down to the crash site. Lots of fire."

"What about casualties?" I held my breath for his answer.

"A cargo jet collided with a small commuter airline. I don't think we have any deaths."

I could hardly believe that. What luck that would be. "Not two passenger jumbos?" I asked confused.

"No, no. A DC-10 and a Navajo."

The trucks, the diesel smell, jet fuel, fire, smoke, lights, noise, people, the wind, the weather, the water. It was an adrenaline high and I loved it.

Dale drove Engine Three into the uneven terrain to get to the crash site. I sat next to him operating the hydraulic turret that had a maximum dispersal rate of 1,500 gallons a minute leaving us two minutes to empty our truck before we had to re-service it. Engine Three was a Walter's 3,000 1971 model. It carried 3,000 gallons of water, 250 gallons of light-water, and 250 gallons of protein foam.

We left the taxiway and drove down a road that field mainte-nance had created so we could get to the crash site. The DC-10 had landed 90 degrees between the runway and taxiway into a small decline.

It was the biggest fire I had ever seen. Flames shooting up 200 feet.

As we approached the fire, I yelled to Dale, "Closer! Closer! Move closer!" He could barely hear me over the truck's pump engines.

I hit the light-water switch to release the mixture of AFFF and water to smother the massive fuel fire; usually a quick remedy except this was a cargo plane with 180,000 pounds of jet fuel.

"Okay, Maggie, but put your face mask down!" Dale hollered.

I was holding onto the hydraulic arm connected to the turret, trying to direct the water stream to the bulk of the fire. "What? What did you say, Dale?"

"Put your face mask down, Maggie!" he repeated. "We're so close to the fire that our front windows are likely to go!"

Maggie working the DC-10 crash. Photo by the Anchorage Fire Department photographer.

I grabbed my mask and pulled it down. I hated the mask. I couldn't see clearly through it. *Had a window ever blown in on a truck before?* That was a nerve-racking thought.

"Dale, move back! Move the truck back!"

He did.

We had our under-truck nozzles on, shooting a fine spray of water to cool the immediate area under the engine. After we emptied the truck of water we maneuvered back to the taxiway to re-service.

Dale connected us with the tanker and I climbed on top of the truck to pour more light-water into the bladder. I anxiously took in the scene, a vision of *Dante's Inferno*. My breath danced in the cold air in front of my face as I stared at the devastation of the crash. Fog and smoke filtered the lights of the emergency vehicles and the massive fire. The twelve-degree temperature, coupled with the ice fog, had caused "hoarfrost" to cling to the trees and bushes, giving almost a winter-wonderland effect, a ghostly contrast.

One of the largest sections of the DC-10 left intact was the tail section. It was wrapped around one of the landing-light towers. The twin-engine Navajo was facing eastbound on Runway Six-Left. The DC-10 had been facing westbound 2,500 feet down the same runway. The pilot started take-off not knowing he was on the wrong runway. The foggy conditions had prevented the tower personnel from seeing him.

When the DC-10 pilot saw the Navajo, he pulled up, severing both wings off the Navajo with his landing gear. The DC-10 then immediately dipped down and crashed.

Because the tower had lost radio contact and couldn't see through the fog, they requested crash crews to respond. At first, they believed it was a 747 and a DC-10. The pilot of a Boeing 737 inbound then reported smoke on the west end above the level of the fog, and the watch commander closed the airport for seven hours. It was amazing there were no deaths or major injuries, just fire and debris. There was total destruction of both the Navajo and the DC-10. The Navajo's nine people on board and the DC-10's three crew members had all escaped with minor injuries.

Still, the raging fire wasn't out. With all six crash trucks on site, including the new Oshkosh 6,000-gallon fire truck, Dale and I returned to the crash site and again dumped our tank. Again and again. Because we had to continuously re-service our trucks and leave the site, the fire flared up each time we left.

Finally, we were able to control the fire within the turret's range, and beyond that we took out the hand lines. I took all 150 feet to go knock down remote fires. I was standing on top of what was left of the DC-10's fuselage, feeling good about the way the rescue was going. Then the wind changed. Within seconds, I was totally engulfed in black smoke and I couldn't breathe. Our head gear was not compatible with air masks, so I wasn't wearing one.

I dropped to my knees and turned off my hose. I had to get out of there! With my hands I started to feel backward for the hose to follow it to the truck.

Dale grabbed me by the collar. "Follow me, Maggie!"

Behind him I edged my way to safety, engulfed in the smoke and fog. I could barely see Dale in front of me as we dragged the hose back over the terrain and debris. As we stood next to the fire engine, I regained some sense of focus.

"Are you all right?" Dale asked, putting his hand on my shoulder. "You want to pack it in? One minute I was watching you; the next you disappeared."

"No, no. I'm good. I'm good." I waved him off. "I'll be all right.

We had been working this crash nonstop for six hours… and I was still wired. I didn't know where my energy was coming from. Soon, however, I would have to go home. My breasts reminded me that I had a hungry baby waiting.

Dale and I continued to work for two more hours. He took the hand line to hit some other hot spots, while I stayed with the engine and monitored the pump pressure.

Suddenly, two co-workers rushed in to get the small ladder from my truck. Dale had fallen into some debris. I trudged with them back through the cargo contents, which were all over the ground, and the ice created from our water. I heard Dale yelling and my heart jumped.

"Dale! Dale!" I shouted.

I leaned over into the wreckage, trying to find him, but I couldn't see him. All I could see was a stream of light-water coming straight at me. The blast hit me in the face and I had to close my eyes. I had switched my fire hood to my structure helmet and my face was exposed.

I blindly searched for Dale. My hands finally felt his upper body. He was on his back. With the light-water still blasting in my face, I pulled him up out of the debris. I could see that he wasn't injured, but the whole nozzle of his hose had broken loose. It had frozen right off and the sixty-pound pressure had forced him backward onto the twisted metal, like a turtle on his back. Relieved because he wasn't hurt, I started to laugh

Then, seeing his frustration, I wiped the light-water from my face, along with my smile.

We worked the fire through Christmas: cleaning up, investigating, and extinguishing spot fires that seemed to burn forever. People gathered to help. Airline personnel, wives and friends brought food and hot drinks to the fire station. A myriad of support came together in the face of the disaster.

To the firefighters, Christmas was all but forgotten as we worked through the night. Then someone – a supervisor, a friend, or a stranger – handed us a cup of hot coffee and said, "Thanks for being here, and Merry Christmas."

In the middle of the night, we stood there, surrounded by the debris of destruction that was consuming our attention. We stood there in our sweat, our physical exhaustion, and our reason for being there. And we simply reply, "You're welcome."

Chapter Twenty-Nine

1985

In mid-December, while working patrol, I was dispatched to the west end of the runways regarding two moose near the active runways. There was a chain-link fence surrounding the perimeter, but the moose always found the "weakest link," an opening on the south side of the airfield. We had an on-going problem with coyotes, ducks, and moose on the runways and it was our responsibility to eliminate any threat that might cause an airplane crash or delay.

When I arrived, Lieutenant Tim Foster, Officer Siegmann, and Officer Dahlberg were already there. The temperature was twenty-three degrees. Tim, in charge of the Great Moose Hunt, advised that he and Siegmann would enter the woods. Dahlberg and I were to patrol the perimeter on foot with our shotguns. If Foster and Siegmann couldn't flush them off the property, the moose would have to be killed on sight. If the moose ran out of the wooded area toward the active runway, Dahlberg and I were to kill them at that point.

Forty-five minutes later and no moose, Lieutenant Foster and Sergeant Siegmann joined us at the road. In another plan of action, Tim had the trooper helicopter sent to our location. The Jet Ranger, housed at Fire Station Two near our location, was already airborne and in our vicinity.

Wind gusts from the rotors stirred up the snow. The pilot, Bob Larson, landed on the road near us.

"Maggie, do you have any blank shells?" Tim asked, his voice rising.

"What?" I got the gist of his question and didn't want to believe it.

He repeated himself, and leaned his face close in to mine. The rotors of the helicopter zoomed overhead.

"No, Tim, I carry only live rounds. Why?" I didn't want to hear the answer. This was something I didn't want to do.

"Because you're going up in the helicopter to scare the moose through the opening in the fence. If you can't do that, we're going to have to shoot them. You have live rounds so be careful Just scare them don't try to hit them."

I thought of my motion sickness and the constant humming and swaying of a helicopter, I could take noise and movement, but not both. I nearly passed out just fishing on a dock.

The helicopter was idling on the road. I ducked and ran toward it. The sensation of being squeezed into a tuna can crossed my mind. I tried to get in the back door gracefully, wearing the police gear in addition to winter clothing. The vibrations from the rotors increased and the pilot, Bob Larson was already heading upward. He smiled at me calmly under his red bushy mustache.

I yelled at him. "Hey, Bob, how do I get this window down?" He pointed to his headset and shook his head of light reddish-blond hair. He couldn't hear me. He pointed toward the back wall and I looked around.

"Okay, okay, I found it." My voice elevated under the engine noise.

I reached back and grabbed the headset. It instantly eliminated the bulk of the outside noise, but I still couldn't hear Bob.

He pointed to the small switch on the volume.

"Okay!" I shouted with increasing nervousness. *This is never going to work.* The volume was already cranked up when I turned it on, and Bob cringed in the front seat.

"Sorry. Bob. Sorry. I've never done this before."

"Maggie," he said with deliberation, "do not shoot the rotors!"

"Well, I hope not. After all, I will be aiming *down*, Bob!"

"Okay," he said, "Pull the window *down*, Maggie."

The window was to my left and I struggled to get it down.

The helicopter swayed from one side to the other, taking my stomach with it, as we cruised above the tree line looking for the moose. "Good grief, Bob, I'm not so sure I won't get sick up here!"

Bob shook his head, thinking he had a real winner in the back seat.

Then I realized I had a major problem with the shotgun. Due to the cramped quarters, I couldn't get the butt onto my shoulder to take the recoil. I shifted my weight several times trying to adjust my body. Had anyone ever shot a shotgun outside the back window of a Jet Ranger? Were there some instructions I should be following?

I spotted the moose and leaned out the window as far as I could without taking a 200-foot fall. I set the shotgun butt against my bicep, the only place it would fit, with a foggy thought of what a broken arm would feel like. I slowly squeezed the trigger and my arm took the full impact. The motion sickness was replaced by immediate and intense pounding pain.

Three more shots, then my arm shook so severely that I couldn't hold the shotgun any longer. Since I couldn't get the moose to move, we returned to the ground.

I stripped the headgear with my left hand. Bob told me to push the window back up. I teetered the shotgun across my lap and struggled to close the window. Bob's patience faltered and he glanced backward, wondering how long this simple task would take me and how much money I was costing the State as the Jet Ranger idled on the road, waiting for me to merely exit.

Finally escaping the helicopter and thanked Bob for the fun and games. I couldn't get out of there fast enough, and hoped my arm wasn't broken.

The four of us hadn't been able to drive the moose through the small opening in the fence. Consequently, they were dispatched.

Standing by my patrol car at the end of the day, even though I knew the meat would go for a good cause, I commented to no one in particular, "Too bad about the moose. I hate to see that happen."

Officer Siegmann said, "Better two moose than 200 people."

Chapter Thirty

1985

For us to train with fire, we needed a fuel source. The State allowed the airlines to dump their fuel wastes into our training pits. This gave us a fuel source, the airlines an area to get rid of their waste, and training cost kept to a minimum.

There was a concern among the firefighters we did not know what we were burning in the training pits. "Recently, the Environmental Protection Agency discovered toxic polychlorinated biphenyls (PCBS) in some of the waste oil at Van Dusen Airport Services, Inc., one of the companies that dumps its waste fuel at the airport." (*Anchorage Times, July 7, 1984)*. Since that discovery, the firefighters were wondering what we were breathing.

"Skydrol, a chemical used in aircraft that becomes toxic when burned, was found in some of the 50-gallon barrels used to store waste fuels, but the airport manager said those barrels were never burned in the practice drills." *(Anchorage Times, July 7, 1984)*

Andy Fowler. I remember him well. He questioned what we were breathing in the fire pits and took a bold stand. He was a young firefighter with the determination to make things safer and a willingness to stand alone. With his dark blonde hair and blue eyes his lean structure did not waver with the thought of being fired. He stood by his principles.

"You know Andy, probably the entire department agrees with you on this effort," I started, "But you'll walk alone in your shoes. You know that?"

"I know, Maggie," Andy's eyes cast downward as we stood in the terminal building, "but I believe in this." And as he raised his intense eyes to catch mine, I could feel his drive for right-ness fueled by anger due to the complacency of the State. Were they even concerned about our welfare?

"You'll jeopardize your employment." I stated, knowing I had often pushed the limits, receiving disciplinary action myself.

"I know. It doesn't matter." His brow furrowed as if to question why I would make such a statement. He was right and I knew it and felt lame for my own lack of strength. Too bad change always seemed to come with such a sacrifice.

Andy was laid-off for an indefinite amount of time for refusing to participate in the fire drills. He had divulged the fact that the department didn't even know what we were being exposed to during our fire training. Until he had a direct answer as to what we were inhaling as we trained to put out fires, he wouldn't coop-erate. I remember that day well as I stood there watching the fire build in the training pits, thinking how much I wanted to sup-port him and couldn't afford to. Although I understood his cause completely, I was still under so much scrutiny myself, I couldn't bear another conflict. Earlier, a reporter had interviewed me regarding this situation and I gave my statement anonymously. Unfortunately, when they aired it that evening on the news, they referred to "she." At that time, there was only one "she." I was scorned by a supervisor who told me do not talk to the press.

I took the wrong avenue and entered the pit drills that day. Only Andy refused to enter the pits that day. In my opinion, he was the only hero that day. After an investigation and EPA was informed, Andy was reinstated.

"Environmental Emergency Services, out of Portland, Oregon, prepared to remove 300 55-gallon barrels of oil, gasoline and combustible solvents from our fire training pits and ship them to Seattle, Washington for disposal. The materials became an issue when about 45 firemen said they were afraid of toxic fumes were being released during the practice fire drills. According to the EPA finding, there were no polychlorinated biphenyls, a substance believed to cause cancer (*Anchorage Times, January 9, 1985*)

From that point forward, we never trained with contami-nated fuels again. I certainly thank you, Andy.

Chapter Thirty-One

Sometimes

Confusion. Sometimes our parents were our protectors. Sometimes they were the predators. Whom could we trust? Sometimes my mom would take us children to a hotel for the night because dad was so violent, fueled by the drinking and constant arguments. Violence, hitting, hurting. Blood.

1985

That May, Tim called me at the house while he was at work. "I've got bad news."

I held my breath.

"They're trying to revise the attorney general's letter to say we can't work together."

He was in line for promotion to captain. Captain Grant had retired four months prior after twenty years and Tim was a candidate for the position of captain. Once again, our world exploded as we were thrown into new litigation.

We retained a personal lawyer and waited. The governor's office was involved, as well as the attorney general's offices in both Juneau and Anchorage were involved, and the administrator to the Department of Transportation, the union, and its lawyer. I knew we had a good case, and I wanted another unconditional waiver.

Including my fights for the locker room, bathroom, and hair regulations twice, then discrimination against marriage, this made my eighth legal encounter involving discrimination. I fell into the stress once again—or maybe I'd never left it.

The position for captain was on hold until this mess could be cleared.

Unknown to us, the State had failed to recognize that we needed a new nepotism waiver *every* time one of us was promoted. When Tim was promoted to lieutenant, he hadn't sought a new waiver, nor did we know we were supposed to. Now, because he was a candidate for captain, the State had recognized its mistake.

The months went by and the strain on our marriage became almost unbearable. Rumors were that I was going to be fired, although I wasn't the one without the waiver, and I had never put in for a promotion. Tim offered to withdraw his name from the promotion list and remain a lieutenant. However, that would not eliminate the problem of our working together without a proper nepotism waiver. So, I pushed him to hang on.

It took ten months for Tim to hit his stress level. Then I agreed to a conditional waiver in the event he was promoted. It stipulated that I could never work another day shift, and neither of us could be promoted. I didn't care about being promoted myself. I was pretty much a line person, although not being able to work the day shift concerned me.

The days when Tim and I had rotated shifts every twenty-eight days, as well as our days off, were long gone. We now rotated shifts by seniority. Being fifth in seniority had put me in a secure position to stay on day shift, with weekends off. While balancing a career with being a mother, this schedule had made the most sense. However, with a conditional waiver that would no longer be an option. If Tim was ever considered for the Chief position, I would have to quit.

Tim and I discussed getting a divorce or my quitting to get around the rule, but I stubbornly refused to do either. It was the principle. So, reluctantly, I agreed to the conditions and Tim was promoted to captain.

Working the graveyard shift allowed a certain amount of time for my mind to wander, whatever that direction might be. Three months after Tim was promoted to captain, I sat in the ramp captain vehicle off Gate 26 thinking about my life. Marriage, career and motherhood. How long could I continue to work the night shift? Was I done fighting? Standing up in what I believed in? Was it stubbornness, selfishness to never give up?

Another foggy night crept into the early morning hours as I reached for my thermos of coffee and poured the steaming black liquid that would help me through another night. At 1:30 in the morning, there was very little traffic, either vehicular or aircraft. In another two hours the sun would begin to spread dawn over the summer day.

Both radios—my Department and the Control Tower—were set on minimum listening mode: low.

The tower operator interrupted my thoughts about my life's direction. "Ramp captain, Ground."

The calmness of the tower operator's voice kept me in check. "Go ahead, Ground."

"Looks like we maybe had a Wien F-27 hit something while taking off on Six-Left. Could you check that out? He said he probably hit something about 150-feet east of the approach."

"Roger, Ground."

I put on my red lights and requested clearance to the west end of the runway. West on the taxiway to the approach end, I asked for additional clearance to check the runway for debris.

"Roger, ramp captain, you're cleared."

I turned left onto the active runway and turned on my spotlight. I didn't know what I was looking for. Just something.

The searchlight, mounted behind the outside left rearview mirror, illuminated sections of the runway beyond my headlights. About one-hundred feet past the approach, I started seeing debris. Not sure what. Then I saw body parts, blood and fur.

I left my pick-up truck and with my flashlight brightened enough of an area to confirm that it was a coyote, chopped up into pieces through the turbo props of an F-27. The tail was the only part of the animal left recognizable.

"Ramp captain, Ground. How are you doing out there?" It had been five minutes or so since I'd had contact with the tower operator.

"Good, Ground. I've got the remains of a coyote. It'll take me a while to shovel it up. Can you give me fifteen minutes?"

"Roger, ramp captain. We don't have traffic on runway six-left for another hour. Take your time."

Knowing I had some time eased my anxiety for being on an active runway. "Roger, Ground. By the way, looks like there's enough here left for a hamburger if you're interested?"

After a spit of silence, the tower operator flatly answered, "No thank you. I've eaten."

I laughed out loud as I stood there alone in the middle of the night in the middle of the largest airport in Alaska.

The fog hid my full view of the chopped-up remains of the coyote. Because I had some time and was alone, I let the sense of scraping bone off asphalt absorb me. Too many times have I been in situations where I deny my emotions—but tonight, I wanted to feel them. Maybe I felt safe in my feelings since the body parts weren't human. Or even knowing I was at the end of my career, I needed to feel that morbid connection.

At the fire station, I threw the remains of the coyote into the dumpster. What I couldn't pick up off the truck bed with my gloves had to be flushed down the drains inside the fire station. So, I backed my rig into a stall. The drain crossed the five stalls. Coming from the darkness, the lights inside the station made me squint.

"Need any help, Maggie?" asked one of the men, opening a door from the kitchen.

"No, I'm good. I just need to rinse off the rig and... well, I'm good."

I couldn't explain to him what I was feeling. I'd done this before in the stalls rinse leftover body parts and blood down the drains. My gloves were soaked in blood.

Even this part of my job I would miss.

Chapter Thirty-Two

1987

In 1987, Tim was being considered for promotion to Chief. The time I had dreaded for so long was facing me. For him to even be considered for promotion, I would have to quit.

I would have to let go of something I loved.

I stood roll call for the last time on April 24, 1987. The men presented me with a dozen red roses and asked me to say something. My throat tightened and my words choked as I thought of my trek from being a nonexistent person into a world where acceptance came—but not without sacrifice. I ran my fingers through a lone deep-red rose. As quickly as the pedals separated, they came together.

My approval into the nontraditional role had come slowly, usually painfully, sometimes humorously. But it did come. It had brought me more insight and understanding than I could have imagined.

Acceptance meant change and change comes achingly slow. Call me idealistic. I naively thought I could slip into this world of tradition and break the rules because I could see beyond them. But it wasn't enough to *see* it. I had to *earn* it.

I stepped into a world of regulations, rules, and past ideas. And dared to dream and believe in my journey. And because of that—the barriers crumbled. The walls came down.

And in my world, it was worth it.

The Department retired my badge and gave it to me on a plaque. I was told, "No one can walk in your shoes."

Epilogue

As the abuse raged around me, I drifted into my imagination—a log cabin in the mountains, a dog, and a .22 rifle. Someday I would find that place. Someday I would find peace.

The packed snow crunched under my boots. My breath hangs in the air before me in the below-freezing temperature.

I arrive at the river and sit on the same log I always sit on. The fallen spruce is a convenient front-row seat of the vast panoramic view. In the wilderness, I feel the serenity for which I searched for my entire life, and I absorb every moment. In my youth I always wondered if I would find this sanctuary away from my days of insanity. I often took a willow stick and drew a picture in the dirt of a cabin in the mountains with a river running by it.

My black-and-white border collie, Toby, prances about, investigating the smells of forest critters. I reach into my backpack for water and relax. On the days that I venture into these woods, a transformation comes over me, like the changing light of the seasons. At this time of year, with the winter air pure and clean, my cobwebs of guilt and self-destructive behavior dissolve. The stark white winter snow against the intense blue sky forced me to squint, downplaying the splendor. Surrounded by the beauty of hemlock and spruce laden with snow, even my worst of memories were held at bay.

Soothed by the gurgling river moving alongside me, I threw a dog biscuit to Toby and watch the ice buildup along the bottom. A million little igloos blurry by the swift water. Thin, jagged ice shards caught in the frigid air in an upward motion.

My feet were beginning to get cold so I stand and stretch, releasing tension. Toby rushes toward me, tail wagging sensing that I was getting ready to leave. I swing my pack over my shoulders and cross the bridge to the road back to the house.

Out of the first winter snow, I step into my little house and feel calm. Within the simple wooden structure, surrounded by birch and spruce trees, a creek meanders quietly through my property and my mind floats softly without turmoil. I can laugh and not remember.

My final roots are here in this small gold-mining community of Hope, Alaska, population 150. At the times I eat at Tito's Discovery Café I recognize every dog on the porch waiting for its owner. And their names.

Age has a way of understanding the past. Sometimes I chuckle at how quickly I used to respond to emergencies, a disaster, and crises. I was attracted to risk-taking, chaos, and danger—an adrenaline high. But my days of arrests, rescues or fire fighting are long gone since I have written this. I didn't write this book to pretend I was some great firefighter or police officer. My stories are light compared to other emergency services. However, being the first woman in the early 1970s entering a close-nit, good ole boys league, was not only a challenge both emotionally and physically, but a reminder of my own fortitude and where I came from.

Thirteen months after I quit the airport, March 1988, my mom died from cancer in the arms of Virginia and Tiger. She never saw my son Josh grow beyond five years old, and she never met my daughter, Brittany, born in 1990.

How simple it was to think, "Your parents don't love you." Through a child's view, it was true. Why else would someone so close to you ....do those things...

In part, it was the times. In part it was the alcohol. And as an adult I know that now. I don't feel any regret, animosity or blame towards them. My childhood gave me the backbone to make a difference in the world. And I thank my parents for that.

My son, Josh, is a firefighter with the Anchorage Fire Department and my daughter, Brittany is a Legal Assistant in Washington. I feel like a relay runner—I ran as fast as I could—then I passed the baton. And let go.

What I do know and acknowledge is my kids are successful, are healthy and did not grow up with the threat of physical, emotional or psychological abuse. My success didn't come in breaking the barriers or setting precedents. My success came in my children. My goal was to break the cycle of child abuse.

And I did that.

On nights during a winter blizzard when gusty winds drive ice crystals against my cabin windows, I watch from safety and feel no consternation. My chin rests in the cup of my hand and remembers a quote from Albert Schweitzer; "One who gains strength by overcoming obstacles possesses the only strength which will overcome adversity."

I wrote for myself. Those who find strength in their weaknesses will find me beside them. They are the survivors.

What matters are fortitude and drive not to give up, ever. And in my world, it's been worth it.

Bibliography

Anchorage Daily News, Tuesday, February 17, 1976: 2 women break male barriers.

Anchorage Daily News, Tuesday, February 1, 1977: Plane crash kills 1.

Anchorage Fire Department, Alaska, James R. Evans, Director of Fire Training: Bringing them out alive. May, 1977.

State of Alaska, The Legislature, HCR 72: Commending members of the Anchorage International Airport Fire Security Section. 1977.

The Anchorage Times, Friday, June 17, 1977: AIRPORT FIRE TEAM HONORED BY GOVERNOR.

State of Alaska, Department of Transportation and Public Facilities: Commendation from the Airport Manager, Mr. Jensen on response to the JA-8054 DC-8 crash.

Anchorage Daily News, Friday, January 14, 1977: 5 crewmen perish. JAL jet crashes here.

Anchorage Daily News, Tuesday, December 5, 1978: Sen. Stevens hurt, wife dies in crash:

Anchorage Daily News, Friday, August 31, 1979: Firefighters face big blaze in airport test.

Alaska Public Safety Academy, Sitka, Alaska, May, 1982: Commendation for Weapon's Proficiency.

The Anchorage Times, Thursday, June 9, 1983: Airport drama. Smooth landing saves plane.

Anchorage Daily News, Saturday, December 24, 1983: Fiery crash on airport runway.

Anchorage Daily News, July 8, 1984: First impressions. Fighting fire with a fiery approach to her work.

State of Alaska, Department of Transportation and public facilities, Anchorage International Airport, February 3, 1984: Commendation from Chief Hynes for coming to the aid of a fellow firefighter during the DC-10 crash.

All mentioned aircraft incidences and crashes that are related in this manuscript have been public information. I have extrapolated some facts from the National Transportation Safety Board's findings.